MW01531339

# The Mental Game
# of Tennis

Master the Mental Side of Peak Performance
and Gain a Competitive Edge!

- For Young Athletes and Beyond -

David J. Fritz

Copyright © 2023 David J. Fritz

All rights reserved.

**ISBN**: 9798863977591

COPYRIGHT PROTECTION WARNING

The author has registered this work at ProtectMyWork.com

The content contained within this book may not be reproduced, duplicated or transmitted without direct written permission from the author or the publisher.

**Legal Notice**

This book is copyright protected. This book is only for personal use. You cannot amend, distribute, sell, use, quote or paraphrase any part, or the content within this book, without the consent of the author or publisher.

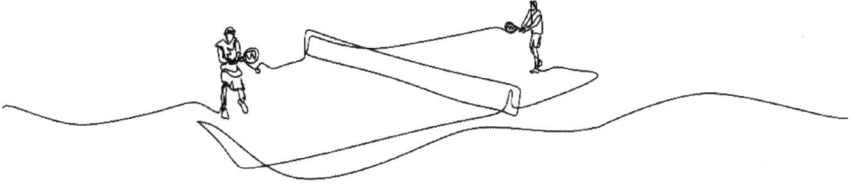

# DEDICATION

*This one's for all you tennis fanatics out there!*

*Whether you're an aspiring pro who dreams of lifting the Grand Slam trophy one day, or an amateur player itching to one-up your game, "Mental Game of Tennis Players" is your playbook. We've crafted this guide to help you tap into the powerhouse that is your mind, to face every serve with confidence and tackle pressure like a champ. It's all about fanning the flames of determination and resilience within you, no matter the odds.*

*So, whether you're prepping for a professional match or gearing up for a friendly set on the local court, grab a comfy chair and let's unravel the secret to a winning mindset. Here's to elevating your game, one mental strategy at a time.*

***Let's hit it!***

# CONTENTS

Introduction by Fabio Lavazza                                               8

Part 1 – Psychology of Tennis                                             12

1 - Diving into Tennis Psychology: Tackling the Devil's Sport            13

Understanding the Unique Psychological Challenges of Tennis              14

Getting into the Mental Demands and Complexities of Tennis               15

Tactics for Handling Mental Roadblocks and Excelling in Tennis          17


2 - The Mindset of a Champion: Cultivating a Winning Mentality           20

Breaking Down the Winning Mindset: The Ingredients of Success           22

Learning from the Best: Acquiring the Winning Mentality from the Pros    29


3 - Set Meaningful Goals to Succeed in Tennis                            33

Techniques for Defining Clear Goals and developing Actionable Plans      35

Tracking Progress and Staying Motivated on the Path to Success          37

Guidelines for setting Effective Goals                                   39

How to Develop S.M.A.R.T.E.R. Goals                                      41

**4 - Overcoming Mistakes: Mental and Physical Strategies for Resilience    44**

Developing strategies to overcome mistakes and bounce back stronger    45

Managing Self-Talk and maintaining composure in high-pressure situations 45

Techniques for Staying Focused and Learning from Setbacks    47

Quick Reset After Mistakes: Bouncing Back Stronger on the Tennis Court    49


**5 - Routines for Optimal Focus and Performance    52**

Establishing Effective Pre-Match and Match-Day Routines    54

Fresh and Funky Idea for Young Guns:    55

Warm-up exercises and rituals to enhance mental focus and readiness    56

Creating Consistency and Maintaining Peak Performance Through Routines 59


**6 - Turning Adversity into Advantage: Thriving in the Face of Challenges    62**

Viewing adversity as an opportunity for growth and improvement    63


**7 - Sports Anxiety Management: Thriving Under Pressure    66**

Coping with public expectations, parental and fan pressure    67


**Part 2 – Mental Toughness Practical Techniques    70**

**8 - Techniques for Improving Mental Toughness in Tennis Players    71**

Boosting Mental Toughness with Positive Chatter and Affirmations    72

Mindset Exercise: The Power of Positive Self-Talk and Affirmations    74

Visualization Power: Boosting Tennis Performance    76

Mindset Exercise: The Art of Visualization    78

Nailing it When the Pressure's On: Techniques for Peak Performance.    86

Techniques to thrive and perform at the highest level under pressure    96

**Part 3 – Best Practices Before and During a Tennis Match**    **99**

Pre-Match Rituals and Techniques in Tennis    100

What to Do During a Tennis Match    102

Making the Most of Breaks    105

About the author    109

Your Free Gift    110

Thank you!    110

# Introduction by Fabio Lavazza

As a professional tennis coach, when I was not coaching professional players, I personally worked with many young talented players who aspired to become tennis professionals.

It is difficult to estimate the total number of young athletes I have met, but I must say I recognized only a very small percentage of them as genuine talent capable of achieving world top rankings.

I have had the pleasure of coaching some of those rare hopefuls throughout my career. Little precocious players of an impressive level: they seemed invincible, competing with players much older than them, capable of beating 3 to 4 older players (which is an achievement for a teenage player). Their fate seemed sealed for future success on the international stage.

However, bitter experience has proven that even the most gifted, strong, and talented athlete can be destroyed by a deadly element, especially among teens and in this sport: their minds, the people's expectations around them, and the continual pressure they have to deal with.

It has become increasingly clear that in professional tennis, where margins of victory are slim and fierce competition is no longer enough for players to rely solely on their physical and technical abilities. To truly excel on the court, a tennis player must harness the power of the mind and cultivate unwavering mental strength from an early age, which is exactly what Mental Toughness for Tennis Players - A Practical Sports Psychology Guide does to help aspiring professional tennis players develop their winning mindset.

This groundbreaking book for aspiring tennis professionals dives deep into sports psychology. It explores the profound impact on the performance and success of young tennis players. Through carefully crafted strategies and techniques, the author highlights the path to developing a winning mindset that can facilitate athletes propelled to new heights.

The writer has particularly focused fundamental importance of mental strength in modern tennis. Unlike the past, when physical size and technical skill were considered enough for competing at the highest level. Today, the mental strength of a player plays a vital role in his or her ability to overcome challenges, adapt to various situations during matches, and stay focused and composed under pressure situations. The book explains how athletes should train their minds to improve focus, turn challenges into opportunities, and ultimately develop a winning mentality needed to succeed both on and off-field.

The book has addressed the critical issue regarding anxiety management and dealing with the intense pressure while being a professional athlete, offering valuable insights and practical strategies to facilitate young tennis players exceed the public's expectations, their families' scrutiny, and their teams' demands.

The significance of developing routines and reasonable goals as essential mental training components has also been highlighted in this impressive book. The writer has delved into the science behind these practices and offered guidance on developing personalized routines and goal-oriented strategies to drive motivation, develop confidence, and establish a sense of purpose while pursuing excellence.

While navigating through the pages of Mental Toughness for Tennis Players, you are about to gain a better knowledge of the essential role sports psychology play in deciding the future of ambitious tennis players. The expert advices and guidance will equip you with all essential practical tools and proven strategies to prmote your mental toughness, combat challenges, and find your actual potential as a tennis player. Get ready to dive into a world where the mind turns out to be the ultimate tipping point, and success is not only due to physical prowess but a proof of your mind's unwavering strength.

Let us discuss how aspiring players can become future superstars!

# Part 1 – Psychology of Tennis

# 1 - Diving into Tennis Psychology: Tackling the Devil's Sport

Welcome to the fascinating world of tennis, a sport famous for its rigorous physical demands, strategic game, and unrivalled mental challenges. The moment you walk onto the court, you join a world that has long been both feared and celebrated—a world named "the devil's sport." Within these lines battles are conducted, champions are produced, and the extent of human flexibility is tested.

In the first chapter we will discuss about psychology of this game (tennis), reveal the complex web of thoughts, empathy, and mental boldness that characterize this game. Tennis is more than simply a physical sport; it is also a mental battlefield in which the winner will be the one who plays with the strongest mindset. A detailed understanding of psychological dynamics specific to tennis will equip you with the essential tools to beat these challenges and emerge as a winner.

We will throw light on the mental challenges that players

frequently come across, such as self-doubt, stress, and attention flaws. By gaining an insight into such challenges, you will learn to step into the psychological battlefield with greater confidence, resilience, and determination.

Also, we will be discussing strategies to get rid of mental obstacles and flourish in this amazing sport. You will learn to how to strengthen your mental game, from handling the power of self-confidence to cultivating mental flexibility.

Hence, as a young tennis player, tighten your seatbelt and get ready to commence an thrilling journey into the bottom of the tennis psyche. We will be unlocking this sport's secrets and paving the way for your victory.

## Understanding the Unique Psychological Challenges of Tennis

In tennis, your mental game is equally important as your backhand or forehand. As a potential tennis pro, you have to recognize its numerous psychological challenges. Tennis could be both thrilling and distressing, thrusting you to the limit and testing your mental strength.

Imagine yourself stepping onto the court, adrenaline pumping, and expectations weighing heavily on your shoulders. It's okay to feel a cocktail of excitement and nervousness. But here's the kicker: All the greats have faced these challenges and come out tougher.

Tennis needs focus, attention, and critical thinking. It demands for quick decisions along with managing your emotions and maintaining a positive attitude—even during terrible situations..

In this part, we will delve into tennis' psychology and find out the specialized mental need it throws at you. You will realize that you are not the only one dealing with those challenges. Many young athletes, like you, have been through a similar mental roller coaster and emerged on top.

Gripping the mental landscape of tennis offer you a competitive edge over your competitors. You will learn how to deal this devil's sport hurdles and convert challenges into opportunities for success and self-improvement. The true goal is to provide yourself with crucial mental tools and approaches that will enable you to give your hundred percent, no matter what the circumstances.

Through a deeper understanding of this mental game, you will find out the key to boost your performance and emege as a winner on the court. While stepping into the fascinating world of tennis psychology, you will find out the practical tehcniques, real-life stories, and valuable insights to facilitate you in conquering the mental aspect of this lovely game. Together, we will outline a course via a mental maze of tennis, encouraging mental strength and flexibility while revealing the success secrets.

## Getting into the Mental Demands and Complexities of Tennis

Tennis demands an active and sharp mind, ability to make split-second decisions, and adapt to the match's flow and ebb. Comprehending the mental needs and complexities of tennis is essential for developing a winning mindset and boosting your game.

Firstly, attention and focus are crucial components of tennis. Staying active and engaged all time actually distinguishes between real champs and chumps. We will discuss strategies and exercises for improving your docus, facilitating you stay focused even during distractions or intense-pressure situations.

Another aspect of tennis' mental game deals with slip-ups and defeat. As most of us know, tennis is referred as a game of highs and lows, and how handling mistakes can significantly impact your performance. We will look into techniques to avoid mistakes, bounce back from defeats, and maintain a positive attitude during the match. Accepting mistakes as growth opportunities and staying flexible and focused during adverse situations are essential skills we will be honing together.

Moreover, decision-making fine art plays a significant role in tennis. Ranging from shot selection to tactical choices, every single decision made by you can affect the match's outcome. We will look into the ways to taking right decisions under intense pressure, while keeping in mind of game situation, evaluating your opponent along with your strengths and weaknesses. Polishing your decision-making skills will transform you into a savvier and smarter player.

Finally, emotion management is a vital component of tennis' mental game. Emotions could be heightend during a match, and it is essential to develop strategies for efficiently controlling and channelling them.

While continuing our reading journey, it is crucial to know that we will be revisiting and revisiting fundamental topics from different perspectives. We intend to provide you with a comprehensive understanding of the winning attitude and optimal techniques you need to succeed in tennis.

This book will serve as your go-to resource for developing the winning mindset you need to realize your full potential, whether you are a devoted young player or an experienced athlete trying to improve your mental game.

In the next part, we will share tips to help you deal with mental hurdles and ultimately transform you into a successful tennis player.

## Remember..

Tennis demands both physical and mental sharpness. Concentrate on your mental game improvement if you desire to perform at your maximum. Delve into the fascinating world of the mind and arm yourself with the crucial resources to tackle mental challenges. If you've got a strong mental game, you'll approach matches with confidence and resilience, paving the road to tennis success.

## Tactics for Handling Mental Roadblocks and Excelling in Tennis

Tennis is filled with psychological hurdles that might hinder your on-court performance. Understanding how to get over these mental obstacles, which range from self-doubt and stress to deviations and pressure, is necessary for succeeding in the sport.

In this book, we will look into various tactics and strategies especially designed to facilitate you slamming your mental roadblocks and expose your complete potential as a tennis player. These techniques will equip you with the mental flexibility to deal with any hurdles promptly.

One of the first steps in tackling mental roadblocks is cultivating a strong self-confidence instinct. We will take a detailed look into the capability of positive self-talk and attestations, guiding you the ways to switch negative thoughts with positive ones and cultivate a self-confident mind. If you trust yourself, you will be better able to handle the ups and downs of a match with confidence and drive.

Tennis can be an emotionally charged sport, and it is crucial to develop tactics for staying calm, composed, and focused during intense moments. You can manage your feelings by doing things like deep breathing routines, visualizing, and practicing mindfulness.

We will help you to understand external distractions including noise and crowd stress to internal factors such as negative thoughts, so that you stay within the game zone and concentrate on what is going on. By learning how to block out distractions, you'll be able to maintain peak performance and make sound decisions throughout a match.

Moreover, we will be discussing the how crucial meaningful goals are and developing a game plan can help you better achieve your goals. Clear goals not only facilitate you to stay motivated but also offers a sense of guidance. We will go through the entire process of setting real and feasible goals and further divide them into reasonable steps. Purusing your goals will develop a sense of management and dedication that will push your tennis journey ahead.

Next, We will share practical exercises, real-life instances, and inspiring stories from great tennis players who conquered their own mental roadblocks. By employing these techniques repeatedly with determination will build the mental strength you need to succeed in tennis.

So, are you all set to embark this game-changing experience? Let's learn the tricks, techniques, and approaches we need to deal with mental roadblocks, reach our full potential, and excel in the "devil's sport."

## Remember..

Handling mental roadblocks requires persistence, execution, and consistency. It is all about dealing with challenges and failures as a chance for development and continual improvement to turn out to be a better player.

# 2 - The Mindset of a Champion: Cultivating a Winning Mentality

Grab your racket, put on your sports face, and get ready to dive into the magical world of mental toughness and a winning mindset. While jumping into a champion's mindset, we are going to reveal the secrets to cultivating a successful mindset that will propel you to new peaks of success both during and after the match.

Imagine you are watching your favorite tennis player in action, effortlessly hitting forehands and skilfully executing precision volleys. You can not help but doubt, "What is making her so distintct? What is the secret to their unwavering success?" Well, it all begins with a positive mindset, my dear friend.

In this chapter, we will be going to understand characteristics that could better define a champion's mentality. We are discussing the resolute confidence that gleam in every shot, the yearning desire for improvement, and the capability to rise after failures. You will learn that building a winning mindset goes beyond hitting the right shots; it's also about perfecting the mental game and bringing out the winner within you.

Now let's hear from one of the greats, the legendary Serena Williams, who once said:

*"I really think a champion is defined not by their wins but by how they can recover when they fall."*

The reality is that even champions are not immune to failure or adversity. They have to deal with lots of challenges and setbacks. But what really makes them standout is their capability to get out of those moments, learn from mistakes, and bounce back stronger.

For a moment imagine all-time greatest tennis players i.e, Serena Williams, Roger Federer, and Rafael Nadal. They didn't become champions overnight. They cultivated a winning mindset through dedication, perseverance, and a fierce belief in themselves. They embraced the process of continuous improvement and never settled for mediocrity. And this is what exactly will be explored in this chapter, i.e., how you, too, could help develop a champion mentality.

We will go through stories of tennis legends, navigate their mindset secrets, and offer you practical approaches for developing your winning mentality. Once we finish this chapter, you will be familiar with all the essential tools to deal with problems, embrace development, and achieve your full potential as a competent tennis player.

**Remember..**

A champion's mindset is not about winning matches only-it's all about loving the journey, learning from mistakes, and enjoying along the way. So let us tie our tennis shoes, develop our aspirations, and light the championship mindset fire inside.

# Breaking Down the Winning Mindset: The Ingredients of Success

When we are talking about acing tennis, it's not all about perfecting your serve or having exceptional physical fitness. These factors are crucial, but there is a secret ingredient that differentiates the true winners from others—the champion mentality. This mental power separates the exceptional from the good, the incredible from just average. Even when technical and physical capabilities are equal, it's the mentality that determines who rises high as the champion.

So, what's in this champion mindset? Imagine a magical integration of self-confidence, strong determination, and a persistent desire to always improve. This continual confidence helps you shines in every situation and decision while being on the court. It is all about turning nerves into excitement, pressure into fuel, and setbacks into springboards for growth.

To nab a winning mindset, you have to start with self-awareness. Take a moment to reflect on your own thought patterns and mental processes, both on and off the court. Do you tend to doubt yourself, or do you have a lot of faith even when things are terrible?? Understanding your mental game's strengths and weaknesses is a must for developing a champion mindset.

Another important characteristic of tennis greats is self-belief—the hidden element that fuels champions. Engage in a positive, uplifting inner dialogue that cheers you on. Swap out self-limiting beliefs with positive affirmations. Celebrate your successes, regardless how small, and take the opportunity to develop a strong foundation for self-confidence.

Having a growth-oriented outlook is another essential part of a champion mindset. Accept progress as a journey, with each setback as an opportunity for growth and learning. Treat failure as a pathway to success rather than a potential stumbling block. Cultivate a passion for lifelong learning and strive to improve daily as a player. Instead of only setting goals based on outcomes, choose goals focusing on the process and self-improvement. A growth mentality will keep you striving for higher standards of excellence.

Tennis can be a wild ride, full of ups and downs. Adopt the "fall seven times, stand up eight" approach. Remember setbacks aren't failures but opportunities to grow stronger and boost your game.

Finally, surround yourself with a team that lifts you and keeps you motivated. Search for mentors, coaches, and fellow players encouraging you to achieve new heights. Tell them about your goals and dreams, and let their help keep you going. Their guidance and expertise will help you cultivate and maintain your "champion mindset."

In the next section, we will emphasize how developing attributes like confidence, determination, and diligence may contribute to cultivating a continual strive for success.

## Remember..

The champion mindset is within your reach. It's a blend of self-belief, a growth-oriented outlook, resilience, and a killer support system. As you cultivate these characteristics, you'll see a transformation not only in your tennis game but also in your life. Embrace the journey, nurture your mindset, and unleash your full potential as a tennis champion. The world's waiting for you to leave your mark on the court.

# Confidence & Resilience: Success Keys

In tennis, most people prioritize physical training and technical proficiency. Countless hours are spent polishing strokes, tweaking footwork, and developing muscular strength. While these things are indeed super important, a key aspect of training is frequently overlooked—mind development. Fostering confidence, perseverance, determination, and a burning desire for success is what genuinely distinguishes the outstanding from the fantastic in tennis.

Imagine this: When it comes to technical abilities and fitness, the two players are virtually identical. They honed their footwork, served perfectly, and mastered their strokes. On paper, they appear to be comparable in every aspect. But, under pressure situations, only the player with a strong and well-trained mindset emerges on top. That's the sheer power of mental prep and how it impacts performance.

It is essential that you set aside time every day to train your mind and include mental training activities as part of your daily practice. Some players may feel that because they're already killing it on the court with awesome athletic prep, they can brush this aspect aside. This will be the biggest mistake, my friend. If you don't try to train your mind, it's like throwing away a powerful hidden weapon. The mind is the command and control center of the complete being.

Consider the golden words from two legendary tennis champions, Rafael Nadal and Novak Djokovic. Nadal once said:

*"At the end of the day, mental preparation is the key. You can have all the essential tools, but you need mental strength to compete at the highest level. Djokovic echoes this sentiment, "I strongly believe success is a lot more than just hitting the ball well. It comes from the mind."*

These legendary players are living proof that the difference between an average player and an outstanding one is a mindset that has been cultivated through the investment of time and effort. They've not only aced the game's physical parts but also devoted themselves to mental training. Their unwavering confidence, resilience in tough times, and determination to succeed drive their excellence.

It's key to realize that the results of mental training may not be instantly noticeable. Unlike physical training, which often shows quick improvements in strength or agility, the effects of mental training take time to show. Due to this reason, most players throw towels during this crucial part of their development. However, the fantastic results attained by Nadal and Djokovic are an attestation to the significance of a nurturing mindset.

Adding mental training as part of your regular routine requires incorporating a variety of different practices and strategies. A few of the tactics you can employ include engaging in positive self-talk, visualization exercises, establishing targets with a methodical focus, and practicing meditation. You can lay the foundation for a powerful mindset that will fuel your success on the court if you devote some training to mental development. This will allow you to maximize your potential in court.

Have got enough of the attributes needed to transform into an exceptional tennis player? I will be sharing some amazing facts about how to develop a positive mentality to foster a successful approach both on and off the court. Let's jump on to the next section!

## Remember..

The mind serves as your secret weapon. It connects your physical capabilities and exceptional performance. By dedicating effort and time for nurturing confidence, adaptibility, determination, and an unstoppable drive for success, you will unlock the actual potential within you.

## Techniques for a Winning Mentality: On & Off Court

Nurturing a winning mentality isn't just about owning the tennis court—it's about ruling every part of your life, shaping your attitude, your actions, and ultimately, your triumphs. Being young proficient player carrying tennis stardom dreams, there are a plethora of techniques you can utilize for cultivating a winning mindset that would serve you well during and after the court.

Are you curious to know the secret tricks the Pros use daily to fortify their winning mindset? Here's a sneak peek at the tactics we're going to dig into more in this book:

**Positive Self-Talk:** Never underestimate the effectiveness of a well-delivered motivational speech, particularly when you are the speaker. Your inner voice has the potential to have significant effects on both your state of mind and your performance. Make it a routine to have encouraging conversations with yourself, replacing criticizing and discouraging thoughts with comforting and motivating ones. For instance, instead of dwelling on a botched shot and thinking, "I'm a total loser," reframe it as, "I'm learning and growing with every point. I'll bounce back stronger." You can build resilience, boost your confidence, and keep that winning mindset by transforming your inner voice into growth-oriented and positive.

**Visualization**: Visualization is a mega tool used by athletes across the board. It's all about conjuring up clear mental images of you acing tennis skills, winning matches, and smashing your goals. Every day, set aside a few minutes of your time to imagine yourself serving with utmost precision, returning shots accurately, and celebrating success on the court. By mentally practicing success, you prepare your mind for top performance and train your subconscious to align with your goals. Visualization boosts focus, confidence, and overall performance, making it a priceless technique for young players dreaming of championship glory.

**Goal Setting**: Setting goals is a core technique for developing a winning mentality. Set both short-term and long-term goals that are specific, measurable, achievable, relevant, and time-bound (SMART). Divide your major goals into smaller, reasonable steps could be handled daily, weekly, and monthly. For instance, your short-term objective may be nailing backhand technique, while your long-term objective might be playing in a top-class junior tournament. Setting your long-term career goals offer guidance, dedication, and a sense of purpose that can boost your determination to achieve success.

**Embrace challenges**: A winning mindset appreciates a great challenge. Instead of fearing tough opponents or tricky situations, view them as opportunities to grow and improve. Seek out demanding practices, play stronger opponents, and push yourself out of your comfort zone. You can cultivate resilience, adaptability, and a thirst for continual growth by stepping deliberately into the zone where you feel the most discomfort. A winning mindset focuses on overcoming hurdles rather than being brought down by them, and one that may be developed by welcoming problems head-on.

**Cultivate a growth mindset**: A growth mindset believes that your skills could be improved with commitment, effort, and a consent to gain knowledge. Adopting a growth mindset means seeing failures and setbacks as stepping stones to success rather than permanent roadblocks. By developing a growth mindset, you create the stage for continual improvement, resilience, and a winning mindset that drives you forward.

In the following section, I will focus on how aspiring young players can adopt a winning mindset from legendary players, and how they can follow them to achieve much-needed mental strength to become pro in their chosen sports. Keep reading!

**Remember..**

Remember, nurturing a winning mindset is totally doable. Tap into the power of positive self-talk, harness the magic of visualization, set SMART goals, embrace challenges, and cultivate a growth mindset. These techniques boost your game on the court and transform you a flexible, passionate, and successful individual in all aspects of life. Dream big and believe in yourself.

## Learning from the Best: Acquiring the Winning Mentality from the Pros

Experiencing the excitement of seeing the pros play is made even better by the opportunity that it offers to learn about the techniques, perseverance, and frame of mind that contributed to their success. You may get inside their thoughts by observing their body language, court-changing routines, and concentration strategy. Once you do this, you can adopt these traits into your game and become more competitive. Let's get right to the point!!

The magic of body language: Watch how the top players in tennis carry themselves on the court—they ooze confidence and authority. Every action they make screams determination and control, delivering a clear message to their opponents that they are in command. Their body language says everything, whether it's how they walk between points, stand during rallies, or react upon winning or losing points. Copying their confident posture and demeanor; you can project a powerful presence on the court and boost your confidence.

**Court-change breaks**: Breaks in service are prime moments for players to gather their wits and regroup. Observe how the pros maximize this time. Some might engage in physical routines like stretching or shaking their muscles to ease tension and keep loose. Others may try boost their confidence by mentally going over their game plan, seeing themselves making successful shots, or engaging in positive mental conversations.

Crafting your own personal court change routine can help you make the most of these pauses, allowing you to reset your mind, collect your thoughts, and approach the next set with fresh focus and determination.

Harness concentration techniques: When it comes to having a strong mental game in tennis, focus is one of the most important factors to consider. Observe how the best players focus on their goals and block out any potential distractions, whether they come from the spectators, their opponents, or their surroundings. They have developed certain routines or reminders that assist them in staying firmly grounded in the current situation. This could be a deep breath before serving, a specific routine of bouncing the ball before returning a serve, or a visual trigger that helps them concentrate on the task at hand. Adopting and practicing these focus techniques can enhance your ability to block out distractions, maintain laser-like focus, and perform your best under pressure.

While we watch the pros and study their mindset, we mustn't forget the power of belief and its massive impact on our tennis journey. Take Novak Djokovic, the juggernaut of men's tennis, who gives us a stellar example of belief's power. Djokovic at the age of 7, boldly announced on a Kids TV show that he will become world's best player. He would have never known at that time his dreams would be realized exceeding all expectations.

Djokovic's strong self-belief has taken him to incredible heights. He not only managed to realize his dreams but became the world's top player and shattered records to place himself among all time best players. Because of his relentless drive and unwavering commitment to the sport, he has been able to maintain his position as the best player in the world for an incredible 378 consecutive weeks.

*"I was dreaming as a kid to be Wimbledon champion, to be No 1 in the world. I achieved those dreams (in) 2011. I wanted more after that. I still want more achievements. Of course I'm driven by the goals. I'm as dedicated to the sport really as anybody else. I obviously know that it's not handed to me, that I have to earn it."*

Reflecting on his journey, Djokovic humbly acknowledges the surreal nature of his achievements. From dreaming of winning Wimbledon and reaching the top of the sport to outshining legends like Steffi Graf, Djokovic's story is a shining testament to the power of setting audacious goals and grinding tirelessly to achieve them.

As budding young tennis players, we can draw inspiration from Djokovic's story. We must understand how to realize our dreams, set career goals, and foster a strong self-belief. We must believe in ourselves like Djokovic and understand that success never comes to us—it's gained through continual hard work, sweat, and a strong self-belief.

So when you watch the pros and marvel at their extraordinary feats on the court, remember that they were once young players with dreams and aspirations just like you. Use these experiences to remind yourself that with perseverance, resilience, and a positive attitude, you, too, can overcome obstacles, face setbacks, and carve your own path to success. Accept the lessons of mental strength, strive for perfection, and never overlook the power of your ambitions. This is a lengthy journey but with the help of positive mindset, you can achieve incredible successes.

# 3 - Set Meaningful Goals to Succeed in Tennis

This chapter will explain how setting goals can turn out a game-changer for serious tennis players. You see, goal setting isn't just some strategy—it's a powerful tool that can carve out a road to success for athletes. We'll get down to the details of why establishing goals is important and how doing so can serve as a road map for athletes to follow on their way to their ultimate goal.

Setting goals that resonate with you is crucial to your growth and performance as an athlete. They serve as a guiding light that keeps your attention on the task and your motivation strong, encouraging you to push beyond your limits and strive for perfection. If you don't have well-defined goals, you'll hopelessly roam around without the passion and commitment you need to realize your full potential.

The process of creating a vision for one's future is the foundation of goal setting. Athletes must envision themselves achieving their long-term objectives and imagine the success they strive for. This vision constantly reminds them of what they're aiming for, fueling their passion and resolve. It keeps their eyes on the prize, even when the going gets tough, as a wellspring of inspiration.

The objective can be divided into two types i.e., long-term and short-term goals. The long-term ones are the big dream you're gunning for, like clinching a major tournament or nabbing a specific ranking. The journey can be broken down into smaller phases by setting short-term goals comparable to the stepping stones that assist you over the river. When you achieve one of your short-term goals, you move one step closer to realizing your long-term ambition.

Establishing your goals brings clarity, helping you prioritize your training and efforts. If you have a certain goal in mind, you can map out your action plan, establish achievable targets, and evaluate your progress more precisely. Athletes stay motivated and determined when they have goals to work for because it helps them realize why they put in the effort daily on the practice field and in matches.

The clear objectives take you out of your comfort zone and takes you to reach new heights. They challenge you to tap into your full potential and constantly up your game. By setting ambitious yet achievable goals, you push your boundaries, fostering resilience, mental grit, and a growth mindset. Every single step toward a goal enhances your skills and drive you closer to success.

So, get that racket ready, grab a cozy seat, and gear up for an adventure in goal setting and achievement. Now it is the time to unlock your potential, stay focused to your passion, and aspire for stars. Note, the journey to athletic splendour initiate with a great vision and ends up with a goal—which motivates you, convince to work hard, and let you feel superior than others. Get started to turn your dreams into a reality? Let's dive into this now!

## Techniques for Defining Clear Goals and developing Actionable Plans

Setting up goals is like loading up your dreams with purpose and direction. Even when the going gets tough, it is the compass that directs you in the direction of victory and keeps your motivation tank filled. In this section, we'll look into the reasons why setting objectives that actually touch your heart is crucial to your athletic journey, as well as how those goals might carve out a path to success for you.

*"The journey of a thousand miles must begin with a single step" Lao-Tzu*

At Roland Garros 2023, legendary champ Novak Djokovic, who has left a lasting impression on the tennis world, once shared some of his eternal experiences with the up-and-coming stars of the game. In his powerful speech, Djokovic underlined the significance of setting goals that resonate and how they've fueled his historic victories. He reminded budding players that winning does not refer to framing titles—its all about your personal evolution and self-confidence that comes while realizing your dreams.

*"And I just want to send a message out there to every young person: 'Be in the present moment. Forget about*

*what happened in the past, future is something that is
just going to happen. But if you want a better future
you create it, take the means in your hands, believe it,
create it'*

While setting your goals, it's crucial to sketch clear objectives. Kick-off by asking yourself what you're really aiming for as a tennis player. Do you want to perfect a specific stroke, climb the rankings, or shine in a particular tournament? By establishing these objectives, you provide yourself with a definite target to strive for as well as a sense of meaning and guidance in your tennis journey.

Once you have achieved your objectives, it's the right time to develop an action plan. Dividing your objectives into smaller, more manageable tasks could be achieved on a daily, weekly, or monthly basis. These steps should be specific, measurable, attainable, relevant, and time-bound (SMART) to keep you on track and accountable.

Tracking your progress is an integral part of goal setting. It gives you a reason to celebrate your wins, no matter how small, and keeps the motivational fire burning on your journey to success. You can use a journal, download an application for tracking your progress, or get in touch with a mentor or coach to seek advice and support. Progress tracking gets valuable insight into your strengths, areas for improvement, and milestones hit, fueling your growth as an athlete.

In this chapter, we'll dig into several strategies for sketching clear goals and mapping action plans that sync with your unique aspirations. We'll additionally find out why it's important to keep track of your progress and maintain a high level of drive, driving insight from the experiences of renowned players like Novak

Djokovic along the way. Therefore, get ready to harness the power of goals that connect with you, ignite the fires of your passion, and go on an adventure involving self-discovery and sporting achievement. The road to success starts with a goal. Ready to step on the gas?

## Tracking Progress and Staying Motivated on the Path to Success

Setting clear objectives that hit home and sketching out action plans is only the start of your journey. To keep your eyes on the prize and maintain your motivation levels on your tennis quest, it's crucial to have a straightforward way to monitor your progress. Here's a simple yet effective method to keep you motivated and hold yourself accountable:

**Craft a Progress Chart**: Begin by creating a progress chart that suits your style. It could be a classic journal, a handy digital sheet, or a nifty mobile app designed for tracking goals. The first step is to identify a specific place where you can track your growth and take account of your accomplishments.

**Pin Down Milestones and Goals**: Break your goals into digestible milestones and targets. These could be weekly, monthly, or quarterly checkpoints that let you measure how far you've come and celebrate your wins. For example, if your long-term career goal is to improve your ranking, you must set a milestone like entering into the top 100 in your area or targeting to achieve certain number of wins in a particular season.

**Keep Tabs on both Quantitative and Qualitative Data**: Monitor both the hard numbers and the soft aspects for a complete view of your progress. Quantitative data encompasses measurable factors like match outcomes, training hours, fitness metrics, and technical skills. Qualitative analysis focuses on the quality of a person's performance, mental stamina, and the consistency of their efforts. Keeping track of both will enable you to evaluate your progress from every possible perspective and identify areas in which you may make progress.

**Pause and Ponder**: Take time for regular reflection on your progress and evaluation of your performance. Evaluate your progress chart and determine whether or not you are meeting the goals and milestones you've set for yourself. Determine if there are any repeating or recurring patterns or trends in your performance, both good and bad. Use this time for introspection to celebrate your victories, acknowledge areas that need work, and tweak your goals and plans.

**Fuel the Motivation**: Integrating several strategies for self-motivation into your daily activities is an effective way to keep the sparks of motivation glowing strong. This could involve visualizing your goals, reading motivational books or phrases, enlisting the support of coaches or mentors, or engaging yourself in a community that is positive and supportive. Find what strikes a chord with you and incorporate these motivational techniques into your everyday life.

**Stay Fluid and Flexible**: As you move forward, you may stumble upon roadblocks or surprise opportunities. Stay agile and ready to tweak your goals and plans on the fly. Remember that challenges/hurdles are part of the journey, and this is how you successfully deal with them, indicating your flexibility and determination.

You will have a crystal clear picture of your journey and the landmarks that you achieved if you use this simple way to keep track of your progress. Your reserve of motivation will be kept full, you will be held accountable, and you will be able to adjust your objectives and strategies as required while you strive for athletic success.

## Guidelines for setting Effective Goals

Setting goals isn't just about daydreaming or choosing random targets; it's about sketching a roadmap to victory. By locking onto the right kind of goals and tackling them with a tactical mindset, you can unleash your true potential and take your game up a few notches. The blueprint we'll dive into is the brainchild of sports psychologists and coaches who've mastered the complex ties between goal setting and sporting brilliance.

1. **Keep an Eye on Process and Performance Goals**: Instead of just fixating on the outcome, zoom in more on process and performance goals. Process goals focus on the nitty-gritty actions and tactics you need to roll out, while performance goals zoom in on personal growth and hitting specific targets. By leaning more towards these goals, you focus on the things you can control that help chalk up a win, rather than just the final score.

2. **Mark Out Clear and Quantifiable Goals**: Stay clear of wishy-washy or too broad goals. Instead, your goals should be specific, measurable, achievable, relevant, time-bound, evaluated and reviewed (SMARTER). So, rather than having a goal like "beef up my serve," opt for something

measurable like "up my first serve percentage by five percent in the next three months." This precision lets you keep a finger on your progress and tweak your efforts as needed.

3. **Strike the Right Balance**: Line up goals that are a bit of a stretch but within reach. Look out for challenges that can take you out of your comfort zone but are still achievable through hard work and dedication. By gunning for realistic yet stretching goals, you gear up for growth and victory without overwhelming yourself or chasing pie-in-the-sky dreams.

4. **Zero in on Positive Goals**: Wrap your goals in a positive package, spotlighting what you're gunning for rather than what you're trying to dodge. Instead of having a goal like "I won't double fault," change it to "I'll consistently nail accurate serves." This optimistic approach directs your attention toward constructive behaviors and fuels a mindset of success.

5. **Decipher Long-term and Short-term Goals**: Have a clear long-haul goal in sight and slice it into tinier, more digestible short-term goals. These short-term goals serve as steppingstones guiding you toward your long-term goal. By setting checkpoints along the way, you can track how far you've come and keep the motivation alive as you inch closer to your end goal.

6. **Craft Personal and Team Goals**: Identify the weight of both personal and team goals. Your individual objectives should align with the roles and duties that you play on the team, and they should also detail the activities you need to

follow to make a significant contribution. The goals of a team center on the collective aspirations of the group and aim to foster togetherness, collaboration, and success. A comprehensive strategy for success can be achieved by balancing these goals.

7. **Differentiating Between Practice and Competition Goals**: Separate practice goals from competition goals. Practice goals include boosting skills, polishing technique, and building consistency. Competition goals, on the other hand, zoom in on optimizing performance in actual matches. By lining up goals for practice and competition, you maintain a wide-angle approach to improvement and maximize your potential in all aspects of your tennis journey.

By sticking to these guidelines, you'll lay a strong goal-setting foundation that hits the bullseye. Keep in mind, goals should be flexible and reviewed regularly to reflect progress and shifting circumstances. By setting crystal-clear, meaningful goals, you'll provide yourself with direction, a motivational boost, and a roadmap to success in your tennis career.

## How to Develop S.M.A.R.T.E.R. Goals

Let's think of a goal as the grand prize or success your hard work strives towards.

**S.M.A.R.T.E.R.** stands for Specific, Measurable, Achievable, Relevant, Time-bound, Evaluated, and Reviewed. It's essentially an updated version of the conventional SMART goal-setting tool, with additional elements to boost the efficiency of achieving your goals.

Let's break down this snazzy acronym so you know what each letter means:

**[S] Specific**: Make sure your goals are crystal clear, neat, and well-outlined. They should answer the "what," "who," and "why" of the goal, giving you a laser-sharp focus.

**[M] Measurable**: To guage your progress and determine whether you've reached your destination, set goals that can be measured.

**[A] Achievable**: Set realistic and achievable goals for yourself. They should push you a bit and demand effort, but they should also be something you can realistically pull off with your resources.

**[R] Relevant**: Your goals should sync up with your overall mission and hold real meaning for you. They should be related to your long-term goals and contribute to your growth and development while also being connected to them.

**[T] Time-bound**: Put a deadline or timeline on your goals. Setting a target date ramps up the urgency and lights a fire under you to get moving.

**[E] Evaluated**: Regularly check your goals to see how you're doing and make any tweaks that might be needed. Routine check-ins help keep you on course and spot any potential speed bumps or room for improvement.

**[R] Reviewed**: Make it a habit to review your goals often to make sure they're still hitting the mark and keeping up with your shifting needs and situation. Reviewing goals allows you to adapt and make changes as you keep growing.

Athletes have the ability to establish clear, actionable goals that are a good match with their dreams and are more likely to lead to a victory if they adhere to the SMARTER goal-setting game plan. It provides a step-by-step technique to develop goals that enable you to stay on track, track your progress, and make any necessary modifications along the way.

# 4 - Overcoming Mistakes: Mental and Physical Strategies for Resilience

In the ever-changing and competitive tennis world, there is always scope for mistakes. From missed shots to unforced errors, every player faces setbacks on the road to success. As a result, champions are willing to bounce back from mistakes, come back stronger, and keep moving toward their goals.

In this chapter, we will be digging into the mental and physical techniques for developing flexibility and mastering the art of bouncing back.

Tennis is a physically and mentally challenging game. Your performance in court will considerably improve as a result of implementing these tactics, and you will cultivate an attitude that perceives challenges as chances for personal development. Understanding the psychology behind mistakes and employing effective strategies can turn setbacks into stepping stones to reaching your full potential.

## Developing strategies to overcome mistakes and bounce back stronger

The ability to learn from one's mistakes and improve as a result is what separates beginners from experts. You are on your way to achieving success and development through your mindset. After you have made a mistake on the court, we're going to discuss some strategies that will help you pick yourself up, get back on your feet, and come back even stronger. You will discover how to turn setbacks into learning opportunities and fuel future successes by practicing self-love and embracing a growth mindset, among other strategies. Let us jump to discuss how self-talk can help you stay calm and composed under pressure situations.

## Managing Self-Talk and maintaining composure in high-pressure situations

When you are in the midst of it, with the game on the line, and all attention on you, being able to retain your composure while handling your internal talk can determine whether or not you are victorious on the tennis court. How you talk to yourself inside your head can significantly shape your ability to recover from blunders and perform your best.

Utilizing positive affirmations is a useful strategy for calming the chaos that you have going on within your head. You can use affirmations as a powerful self-talk tool to block out negative or self-doubting ideas. By consciously selecting uplifting and encouraging words, you can reshape your mindset and build rock-solid self-belief.

For example, rather than permitting negative thinking, such as "I always choke when the pressure is on" control your thoughts and replace it with a positive affirmation like "I shine in tough spots and give my best." By repeating these positive thoughts on a consistent basis, you are retraining your brain to concentrate on your qualities, ability to recover, and previous wins. This shift in inner chatter gears you up to face high-pressure situations with a positive mindset, allowing you to stay cool and deliver top performance.

Another helpful tactic for controlling your inner dialogue is to give yourself a pat on the back for your strengths, victories, and improvements. Reflecting on your skills and accomplishments is a powerful booster of your abilities, even when the heat is on. For instance, before a crucial point or a difficult match, remind yourself of your skill set, the sweat you've put in, and how far you've gone. This will help you stay focused and at peace.

Putting these tricks into action needs practice and persistence. Make positive decisions as part of your everyday routine both within and out of the court. Repeat them to yourself before practices and games, as well as whenever you find moments of self-doubt. In addition to this, make it a regular practice to consider your achievements and the good things in your life. Write them down, maintain a journal of gratitude, or discuss them with your basketball coach or your cheering team. The more you employ these tactics, the more efficiently they'll help you control what's going on inside while retaining your composure under pressure.

### Remember..

Remember that managing your self-talk is an ongoing process. It's important to be patient with yourself and stay committed to positive mental habits. You could give yourself an invaluable resource that will enhance your self-esteem, relax your anxiety, and assist you to thrive at your greatest during the most challenging times of your tennis career by developing a constructive internal conversations.

## Techniques for Staying Focused and Learning from Setbacks

Obstacles are frequent in tennis' thrilling rollercoaster ride. But keep in mind that your progress as a player isn't influenced by your mistakes but instead by how you recover from them. It's vital to develop talents that enable you to maintain your focus, learn lessons from challenges, develop adaptability, and ramp up your game.

> Obstacles are frequent in tennis' thrilling rollercoaster ride. But keep in mind that your progress as a player isn't influenced by your mistakes, instead how you recover from them. It's vital to develop talents that enable you to maintain your focus, learn lessons from challenges, develop adaptability, and ramp up your game. "Success is not final; failure is not fatal: It is the courage to continue that counts." - Roger Federer

Mindfulness is a useful tool for maintaining incredibly sharp focus.

It is all about being fully aware of your thoughts, feelings, and sensations without passing judgment. You can teach your brain to ignore interruptions, concerns, or depressing ideas by integrating mindfulness into your game.

Turning slip-ups into learning opportunities requires a growth mindset. Understand the fact that mistakes are simply opportunities for development rather than failures. Instead of focusing on errors, use them as starting points for improvement. Analyze the issues that came up, identify the takeaways, and identify precise actions for dealing with those issues. With a growth mindset, stumbling blocks turn into stepping stones that push you forward in your tennis journey.

Last but not least, talking to an experienced coach, mentor, or sports therapist can be a game-changer, providing invaluable guidance and support in recovering from setbacks. They can guide you through crafting effective coping strategies, provide unbiased feedback, and share tailored techniques to up your mental game.

You may improve your capability to stay focused, learn from mistakes, and continue developing into a psychologically tough tennis player by embracing mindfulness, encouraging self-communication, an evolving mentality, and expert guidance.

These strategies, when applied consistently, will boost your mental resilience and fire up your on-court performance. Let's look more closely at these strategies so that you'll be prepared to overcome hurdles and succeed in your tennis career.

## Remember..

Every tennis legend has made mistakes and encountered hurdles.

Their approach to these issues distinguishes them. You'll develop the resilience required to overcome whatever stands in your way by learning techniques for bouncing back from blunders, controlling inner chatter, retaining composure, and viewing setbacks as stepping stones. So, let's dive headlong into these strategies and equip you with the mental and physical tools to bounce back from goof-ups stronger than ever!

## Quick Reset After Mistakes: Bouncing Back Stronger on the Tennis Court

We all goof up from time to time - it's part of the game. But how players react to those blunders is what genuinely changes the game. This chapter will discuss the effectiveness of the quick reboot approach and how it could dramatically improve your performance.

Mistakes are often seen as stumbles, moments of "doh!" on the court. However, guess what? They could also offer amazing opportunities for personal growth and learning. Dwelling on those missteps can trip up your focus and self-belief, throwing off your next shots and your game. Therefore, maintaining calmness and recovering promptly in the midst of battle necessitates developing a rapid reset mentality.

Take Roger Federer, one of the tennis GOATs. He's famous for his ability to bounce back fast after fumbles. Known for his elegant playing style and mental grit, Federer shows an extraordinary knack for shaking off errors and zeroing in on the next point. Federer possesses the ability to recover from defeats and poor performance without losing his temper.

## Rapid reset tricks of the trade:

There are a bunch of tactics players can use to recover quickly from slip-ups. One handy hack is to develop a ritual or routine between points. Taking a deep breath, visualizing yourself making a basket, or giving yourself a pep talk. By focusing on the current moment instead of your mistake, these rituals help you face the next phase with a new perspective.

Another tactic is to stay in the moment and keep your focus razor-sharp. By totally immersing yourself in the current point and shaking off past slip-ups, you can stop those missteps from lingering in your head. Concentrating on feeling in a particular body part, such as the soles of your feet, is an excellent way of increasing this practice.

By shifting their focus to the physical sensations in their feet, players ground themselves in the now. They learn to recognize the slightest hints of stability, balance, and relationship with the court. By grounding themselves in the present moment through this mindfulness practice, players can shrug off any leftover frustration from past slip-ups and zero in on the task at hand.

Concentrating on your feet and their connection to the ground also boosts a sense of stability and solidity, building confidence and calm. It serves as a kind reminder that every achievement signifies a fresh beginning and the opportunity to succeed.

To use this tactic, players can take a moment between points or during changeovers to intentionally shift their focus to their feet. As they ready for the next rally, they might deliberately scan their senses, noting the stress, balance, and slight shifts. Players may develop a solid foundation that allows them to let go of past mistakes and be completely in the present by consciously looking at their feet and the ground under them.

By weaving mindfulness and focused attention on the feet into their game, players develop a heightened sense of being in the now and the ability to bounce back quickly after slip-ups. This tactic not only beefs up their mental resilience but also deepens their connection to the game's physicality.

Tennis players who are interested in achieving their greatest potential must have the willingness to bounce back promptly from mistakes. A rapid-reset mindset is crucial for dealing with failures and improving your performance on the court, whether you're designing it after world-class players like Roger Federer or developing your own rituals. Remember, every point is a new chance to show your stuff, and with a quick reset, you can bounce back stronger than ever!

# 5 - Routines for Optimal Focus and Performance

Every second counts in the relentless mental game of tennis. Keeping your focus and playing at the top of your game could make a huge difference.

In this chapter, we're going to unpack the art of crafting kick-butt routines that will crank up your performance both on and off the court. Routines are effective game-changers that help you focus, hone your attention, and get prepared to kill it by bringing order to the chaos. Whether it's setting pre-match rituals or working in specific warm-up moves, this chapter will lead you on the journey to mastering routines that will launch your game to new heights.

Understanding the importance of pre-game practices is essential for athletes because it illustrates how a well-planned routine may pave a path for a stellar performance.

Athletes can identify rituals and actions that will ignite their right mental state, such as envisioning the victory, performing dynamic stretches, or ramping up some pump-up music, and then develop a personal routine that complements them like a glove.

On top of that, nailing down a regular warm-up routine that blends with specific exercises to prep both body and mind is crucial. This integration of physical and mental prep sets up for a top-notch performance and ensures that athlete's step into the game focused, cool, and ready to slay.

For top-notch success on game day, honing both your intellect and body is critical. Athletes may achieve a higher level of concentration and effectiveness through applying rituals, whether they are lucky charms or planned moves. Mind hacks like visualizing, positive self-talk, and deep breathing play a big role in preparing your mind for the challenges ahead.

Keeping nerves and anxiety in check is also key, and athletes can use strategies like progressive muscle relaxation and mindfulness techniques to stay cool. Athletes create a solid foundation for success and optimize their potential on the field or court by incorporating those elements into their pre-game routine.

Consistency is the secret sauce to unlocking peak performance in tennis, and crafting effective routines is the road to getting there. Routines offer stability, familiarity, and a solid base for laser focus and top-notch performance. Athletes can maximize their physical and mental planning, overcome interruptions, and achieve flow where they might perform at their highest level by using the power of persistence. They might adjust their strategies to meet the unique challenges they experience by adapting practices to fit different circumstances. By continuously fine-tuning schedules, players can stay in tune with evolving needs and ambitions.

## Establishing Effective Pre-Match and Match-Day Routines

Rituals are the magic recipe for unlocking top-notch focus and performance in any sport where keeping your head in the game is key. They provide a consistent routine for young players to rely on, helping them to enter every situation with a zen-like calmness and can-do attitude. The importance of creating excellent pre-game and game-day schedules, including warm-ups and practices that boost your mental concentration and preparedness, will be explored in this chapter. We are also going to let you in on a fresh, creative idea that young players can use to send their game into orbit. Strap in and get ready to learn the art of routine and how it can make champions.

Picture a young tennis player just starting their climb to the top. They idolize the legendary Serena Williams, who is recognized for her fierce resolve and laser-like attention on the court. Fired up by Serena's killer preparation, the young player decides to weave a unique routine into their pre-match ritual. Instead of just knocking balls around on the practice court, they lean into a visualization exercise. When they close their eyes, they imagine themselves hitting flawless serves, booming groundstrokes, and agile footwork. Every element is perfectly represented, including the sound of the ball striking the strings and the cheers of the spectators after a winning score. Their trust as well as relaxation, are enhanced by this visualization process, which carries over into their real matches.

Rafael Nadal, regarded as one of tennis' greatest players, is recognized for his unrelenting dedication and diligent routines. Before every match, Nadal sticks to a carefully choreographed routine that includes a unique warm-up drill called the "shadow swing." This move involves mimicking his groundstrokes and footwork without a tennis ball, letting him fine-tune his technique and really get into the groove of his game. By incorporating this cutting-edge warm-up into his regimen, Rafael Nadal is able to increase his muscle awareness and mental acuity, ensuring that he enters each match with a rock-solid foundation.

## Fresh and Funky Idea for Young Guns:

To put some extra oomph into their routines, young guns can dive into the world of personalized rituals. These rituals can be as straightforward as wearing a lucky charm or chanting a motivational mantra before stepping onto the court. A young player could, for instance, decide to wear a unique bracelet that holds their memories and represents their commitment to the sport. Their purpose is reaffirmed by this ritual, which also fosters a sense of ease and familiarity that may help them feel better mentally.

Young guns develop the foundation for exceptional play by incorporating personal practices into their routines, bringing an extra layer of dedication and purpose to their game.

## Remember..

Considering figuring out which strategies work best for every specific player is an essential component to building efficient routines. Develop a routine that's effective for you and allows you to perform to the best of your ability on the court by testing with various routines, practices, and personal touches.

# Warm-up exercises and rituals to enhance mental focus and readiness

In the realm of tennis, warm-ups and rituals are like the pre-game pep talk for your mind and body, priming you for a top-notch performance. Create your own inventory of creative workouts and routines to hone your mental concentration and readiness as developing players striving for the top. This part focuses on the primary routines of Rafael Nadal, the king of clay, as well as some new and innovative warm-up exercises. By weaving these techniques into your routine, you can ramp up your mental state and be raring to go for a killer performance on the court.

## Creative warm-up exercises

**Mindful Movement Flow**: Start out your warm-up with a mindful movement that synchronizes movement with breathing. This might be a flow of yoga poses, powerful stretches or even tai chi-inspired movements. You can awaken a keen awareness of body consciousness and be mentally ready for the battles ahead by listening to what is happening right now and the vibes in your body.

**Quick Draw Drills**: Dive into drills that give your reflexes and mental agility a workout. Add exercises that require quick reflexes, such as striking a ball against a wall and making on-point shots in response, or focus on quick footwork patterns. These drills don't just boost your physical coordination but also train your brain to make lightning-fast decisions under the gun.

## Rafael Nadal's mental focus rituals

Rafael Nadal, who is recognized for his mental strength and laser-like focus, has created rituals that enhance his mental state prior to and during matches. His practice of placing his water bottles and towels in specific places is one of his noteworthy habits. This small act lets him carve out a sense of order and control in his environment, fostering a focused and cool-headed mindset.

Besides, Nadal has a ritual of tweaking his shorts and tugging at his shirt before serving. This action acts as a trigger, driving him into a state of complete focus where he blocks out distractions and puts all of his energy into each shot. These rituals not only improve Nadal's attention but also provide him with a sense of comfort and ease, which may evolve the course of a match under pressure.

Looking at Nadal's rituals, you see that they work because they anchor his mind in the now. Nadal establishes a psychological state that fosters focus and mental sharpness by making precise physical movements and creating a sense of discipline. As young players, you can tweak and personalize these rituals to suit you, finding unique gestures or actions that act as cues to flip into a focused and ready mindset.

## Crafting your own ritual

Developing your own focus ritual as an inexperienced player can significantly improve your performance on the court. You can begin a routine to give your body and mind an effective signal that it's time to pay attention and get ready for the game to begin. Here are a few ideas to consider:

1. **Choose a symbolic move**: Find a small, meaningful move that resonates with you. You could modify your wristband, take a deep breath, or touch your racket's strings. This motion can serve as a physical catalyst for a mental move, enabling you to block out external factors and focus all of your mental attention on the game.

2. **Craft a routine**: Set up a pre-match routine that includes specific moves and rituals. Exercises in visualization, encouraging self-talk, and physical warm-ups can all be a part of this routine. Consistently following this routine before each game builds a sense of familiarity and confidence that helps you slide into a focused mindset.

Just remember, the goal of warm-up exercises and rituals is to nurture a rock-solid mind-body connection, boost confidence, and dial up mental focus. Learn how various exercises and rituals influence your frame of mind and your efficiency on the court by trying them out. You can prepare for a stellar performance through incorporating unique warm-up exercises and personal focus routines into your daily routine.

Draw inspiration from the rituals of tennis legends like Rafael Nadal, but don't forget to craft your own rituals that jive with your personality and playing style. Use your imagination to make your routine for warming up, representing your distinct style and personality as a tennis player.

# Creating Consistency and Maintaining Peak Performance Through Routines

If there's one thing that makes or breaks a tennis player's game, it's consistency. The capacity to continually perform at an outstanding level, and improve after every game is what differentiates champions from the rest. Carving out robust pre-game and match-day routines, plus blending in warm-up drills and rituals, not only amps up your mental focus and readiness but is also key to crafting and keeping up consistency in your game. This section will reveal the secret to consistency, demonstrate how to personalize it, and explain how routines can help you focus and concentrate on the court.

---

*"Consistency is the bridge that connects practice to mastery. It is the key ingredient that transforms talent into success on the tennis court." - Andre Agassi*

---

## The magic of consistency

Consistency is like the confidence and stability glue of your game. When you can consistently pull off your shots, tactics, and strategies, you build a rock-solid base that lets you effectively handle any game situation. Additionally, consistency reduces mental and emotional rollercoasters, enabling you to stay composed and focused despite the highs and lows of the game. You may reach your goals and perform at your best owing to this capacity for continually bringing your A-game.

## Crafting consistency through routine

Craft your pre-game routine: Create a pre-game schedule that you adhere to diligently before every game. The routine should include particular movements to get you in the appropriate frame of mind, mental preparation techniques, and physical warm-ups. By creating a pre-game routine, you establish a planned and comfortable series of actions that indicate to your body and mind that the game is about to commence.

Maintain your game-day pattern: Create a game-day routine that will help you perform at your best. A healthy breakfast, visualization exercises, a review of your game plan, and relaxing activities like enjoying music or practicing meditation can all be included in this regimen. Maintaining a consistent routine on game days allows you to feel at home and mentally prepared, ensuring that you reach the court with a focused and composed attitude.

## Woven into your game

Build rituals as triggers: Weave specific rituals into your routines that act as triggers for your focus and concentration. These can be simple tasks like counting the bounces of the ball before serving, taking a deep breath, or imagining a successful stroke. These rituals act as anchors that reel your attention back to the now and help you shut out distractions, cranking up your focus and concentration during clutch moments.

## Practice with purpose

Make practice sessions a regular part of your routine. Approach each practice with a clear aim and set specific goals to work on. You build the muscle memory and mental flexibility required for consistent performance through regular practising. Games reflect what happens in practice.

Consistency is a power player behind tennis success. By crafting effective pre-match and match-day routines, blending in warm-up drills and rituals, and weaving routines into your game, you can lay a rock-solid foundation of consistency in your performance. Being consistent helps you overcome difficulties on the court and give your best effort, game in and game out. Consistency also fosters confidence, strength, and resilience. Harness the power of routines, make them a crucial part of your prep and gameplay, and watch your performance rocket to new heights of excellence.

In next section, we will discuss how to transform hurdles in your favor. Keep reading!

# 6 - Turning Adversity into Advantage: Thriving in the Face of Challenges

We are frequently put to the test by surprises and hurdles in life, tennis, and just about any sport. But here's the juicy bit: champs aren't born from dodging difficulties; they're shaped through their power to rise above them.

It's not an innate ability only possessed by the exceptional; rather, it's a mindset and a set of strategies you can develop. Tennis psychology is crucial in enabling you to navigate chaotic waters and emerge stronger.

Always remember, it's not about sidestepping the tough stuff, it's about hugging those challenges and flipping them into advantages. So, whenever you have a failure, consider it as an opportunity to advance, appreciate yourself, and take it as an entry point for your psychological and emotional growth. You will overcome problems and discover your fullest potential wherever you are on the court when you have the right mentality and approaches.

Patrick Mouratoglou, a top-notch tennis coach, hit the nail on the head:

*"Success is not final, failure is not fatal: it is the courage to continue that counts."*

Hug those challenges, learn from them, and keep moving. This is the first step towards becoming a powerful, competent, and successful tennis player.

## Viewing adversity as an opportunity for growth and improvement

It's not a question of whether you'll encounter a challenge in the competitive and nasty world of tennis; it's about when. Your strategy and response to these tests will really determine how successful you are as a player. Instead of looking at obstacles as setbacks, start seeing them as golden opportunities for growth and improvement.

Let's think about Serena Williams, the legend herself. She has endured a variety of adversities throughout her career, including injury, legal issues, and heartbreaking defeats on the court. What sets Serena apart, however, is her knack for turning rough patches into motivation and fuel for success.

Serena uses a growth mentality in tough situations. She views difficulties as opportunities to identify areas that need improvement and hone her skills. Instead of stewing over a defeat or setback, she zeroes in on dissecting her performance, spotting where she needs to up her game, and carving out a plan to get better. This mindset is her secret to continual growth and staying on top.

Start by changing the way you perceive challenges if you want to apply this approach to your own tennis path. Instead of perceiving them as bad experiences, consider them as opportunities to grow, change, and challenge your capabilities. Frame challenges as opportunities to pinpoint your strengths, weak spots, and growth areas.

A handy strategy for reframing challenges is to keep a journal or reflective diary. After every competition or practice, try a few seconds to note down the challenges you faced, the lessons that you obtained, and the actions that you may implement to get better. This practice might help you with diving deeper into your achievements and establishing your plan for future development.

Another solid tactic is to seek the wisdom of a sports psychologist or mentor who knows tennis inside and out. These pros can offer precious insights, mental tools, and strategies to help you overcome adversity and keep a resilient mindset. They may demonstrate strategies like imagining, positive self-communication, and accomplishing objectives to assist you in handling hurdles and perform your best game.

## Remember..

A competent tennis player is identified not by the lack of challenges, but by their capacity to turn setback into opportunities for growth. Use adversity as an opportunity to learn, improve and become a more resilient player. A great advice from Arthur Ashe, renowned tennis player and a human rights activist: " Begin wherever you are. Employ what you got. Do what you can." Hug the challenges, stay determined, and squeeze every opportunity for growth and improvement on your tennis journey.

# 7 - Sports Anxiety Management: Thriving Under Pressure

Let us dive into the intriguing world of sports anxiety management, where athletes learn the art of thriving when the heat's on and give their performance that extra kick on the big stage.

In this chapter, we're going to delve into the twisted maze of handling the mind games that come with public scrutiny, the pressures from mom, dad, and fans, and the butterflies fluttering in your stomach before a major showdown.

By exploring successful strategies, we strive to offer athletes the strategies and tools needed to bring their best game regardless of whether the spotlight becomes overwhelming or the pressure escalates.

Participating in sports demands more than mere physical aptitude; it additionally necessitates mental strength and perseverance. Dealing with the pressures to meet the crowd's expectations, the weight of your parents' hopes and fans' dreams, and the jitters that accompany a major event can make an athlete's brain spin. Realizing how to cope with those issues and turning them into your favor is critical for any striving athlete.

# Coping with public expectations, parental and fan pressure

The most challenging part of an athlete's path involves managing the pressure of parents and fans as well as the expectations of the public, which is frequently linked with anxiety and mental health issues. The moving story of Mardy Fish, a former pro tennis player, gives us a revealing glimpse into the toll these pressures can take.

Mardy Fish's ascent in the tennis world was nothing short of a meteoric rise. He flew up the ranks with his powerful serve and quick footwork, winning the respect and amazement of both fans and experts. The weight of public expectation increased along with the number of his victories.

With each win, anticipation for his next match skyrocketed. Fans sat on the edge of their seats, hungry for more stunning displays of athleticism and skill. Expecting nothing less than brilliant, his parents, instructors, and sponsors set their hopes on him. While these expectations can fuel some athletes, for Fish, they were a lead weight.

As the pressure ramped up, Fish started grappling with increased levels of anxiety. He started experiencing psychological problems due to the pressure of hopes and the anxiety of dissatisfying those who had believed in him. The sport he once loved started to feel like a vice, as anxiety cast a dark shadow over his every move on the court.

The turning point in the sport happened at the 2012's US Open, one of the most renowned tennis tournaments. As Fish geared up to face Roger Federer, a wave of panic swamped him. His heart pounded, his breaths came in gasps, and he felt a sense of doom. He couldn't handle the degree of his anxiety, so he took the difficult decision to step away from the competition, which shocked the tennis community.

This turning point ignited Fish's resolve to face his anxiety head-on. Knowing that his mental wellness was equally crucial as his physical well-being, he requested professional help and went on a daring journey of self-discovery and rehabilitation. Through therapy, he got a better grip on his anxiety triggers and learned techniques to manage and tackle the pressures he faced.

Fish's road to recovery was filled with speed bumps. It took enormous courage to confront his mental health issues in a world where showing vulnerability is often seen as a weakness. But by sharing his story, Fish not only found comfort and support but also became a beacon of hope for others wrestling with similar demons.

Fish continues to champion mental health in the sports world. He's all about breaking down the stigma around anxiety and encourages athletes to make their mental well-being a priority. His story serves as a reminder that seeking assistance is not a sign of weakness but rather a strength and that confronting mental health issues is a crucial aspect of an athlete's career.

It's critical for prospective tennis players to understand that the demands of social demands, parental pressure, and audience pressure can fuel anxiety. Recognizing anxiety symptoms and getting the right support is vital for effectively managing and navigating these challenges. Communicating publicly about mental disorders can assist in establishing an appropriate environment for open discussion while minimizing the degree of social exclusion that many players encounter while battling mental health issues.

Also, adopting coping strategies that cater to your unique needs can help athletes manage performance anxiety. Deep breathing workouts, visualization techniques, constructive self-talk, and mindfulness exercises are a few examples of these strategies. Building a robust support system of coaches, family, and friends who understand and empathize with your struggles can also provide much-needed guidance and moral support.

Mardy Fish's story serves as a potent lesson that mental health is just as crucial as physical prowess in sports. Athletes can foster resistance while developing a foundation for long-term success by recognizing and dealing with anxiousness and other mental wellness challenges. Embracing vulnerability, seeking support, and implementing strategies to manage anxiety is key to acing pressure situations and enjoying a fulfilling sports journey.

# Part 2 – Mental Toughness Practical Techniques

# 8 - Techniques for Improving Mental Toughness in Tennis Players

Welcome aboard the journey to mental toughness in tennis! In this section, I will share many useful tips and tricks to help you develop your mental strength, improve your performance, and handle on and off-the-court challenges with great confidence and intelligence.

This chapter includes a comprehensive armor of tactics for strengthening your mental game, from giving yourself a good motivational talk to visualizing your victory, calming using relaxation techniques, and discovering your peace with mindfulness and meditation. By putting these techniques to work, you'll ace your focus, handle pressure like a pro, pump up your confidence, and leap over any hurdles that are emerging during games.

We will be digging into how each technique specifically applies to the tennis universe, dishing out practical examples and guidance to make sure you get it right. These helpful guidelines can help you to reach your optimum potential, boost your game, and perform at your best, irrespective of how proficient you are with a racket.

Always remember developing mental toughness is a remarkable journey that demands consistency and resilience. The techniques we'll talk about in this chapter aren't magical quick fixes but rather tools that, when woven into your training routine, can help you foster a resilient mindset that'll have your back both on and off the tennis court.

## Boosting Mental Toughness with Positive Chatter and Affirmations in Tennis

Have you ever had a chat with yourself? This is something that everyones does. It is called self-talk or self-communication. This internal chitchat has a big impact on how we think, feel, and finally act. By cranking up the volume on positive self-talk and using a neat trick called positive affirmations, you can supercharge your confidence, focus, and overall mental toughness on the tennis court.

Self-communication and positive affirmations are revolutionary strategies in high-stakes tennis sport. The way we chat to ourselves in our heads can totally change our mindset, boost our confidence and improve our court performance. Realizing the significance, it is to develop a garden filled with positive affirmations and inspiring self-communication is vital for every tennis player hoping to attain their maximum potential.

The fact is, affirming thoughts and constructive feedback have value because they affect our perspective. The thoughts we keep repeating to ourselves dig their way into our subconscious and sway our beliefs and actions.

By consciously choosing to pep-talk ourselves with positive, uplifting phrases, we can reset our minds to spotlight our strengths, talents, and potential for success. This mindset shift bulks up our self-belief and confidence, giving us the guts to face challenges head-on with resilience and determination.

There are several benefits to incorporating strong self-talk and positive affirmations into your tennis routine. They start by putting an end to self-doubt and negative ideas. When you're faced with tough spots or stumbles, having a stockpile of feel-good phrases lets you shift your focus and direct your energy towards solutions and getting better. Moreover, utilizing constructive self-talk enhances mental toughness, allowing you to comeback from errors and maintain patience under pressure.

Better focus and concentration on the court can also be achieved by practicing positive affirmations and self-communication. You develop a mental environment that fosters clarity and top-notch performance by exchanging constructive and positive thoughts for self-criticizing or distracted ones. This boost in focus helps you make better calls, nail your shots with precision, and stay fully in the zone in every game moment.

Being persistent and determined is essential if you want positive affirmations and self-talk to be effective for you. Determine any personal constraints or negative thoughts that may be hampering your efficiency, to begin with. Take these beliefs head-on and replace them with positive phrases that sync with your tennis goals and values.

Create your own affirmations that ring true for you and stir up strong emotions. As a routine, athletes say these words before games, warm-ups, and practices. Picture yourself with the qualities and results you're after and back up your affirmations with vivid mental images.

Also, tune into your self-talk during games and competitions. When you catch yourself sliding into negative or self-critical thinking, consciously flip the script into positive and constructive thoughts. This requires a significant level of consciousness and self-awareness, but with practice, it will turn into a habit that will have a major influence on your performance.

## Mindset Exercise: The Power of Positive Self-Talk and Affirmations

### Step 1: Identify Negative Self-Talk

Begin by becoming aware of your internal dialogue during practice and games. Be mindful of all times when you have self-doubt, critical thinking, or negative ideas. You may discover recurring themes or patterns in your self-talk.

### Step 2: Create Positive Affirmations

Once you've identified the negative self-talk, consciously create positive affirmations to counter them. These should be encouraging affirmations that align with your tennis objectives and core principles. They should invoke strong emotions and give you a sense of empowerment.

For instance, you may contradict the idea, "I always miss my serve" by stating, "Each serve I take is my chance to hone my skills, and I am feeling progressing with every single one."

## Step 3: Practice the Affirmations

Integrate these positive affirmations into your tennis routine. Repeat them during practice, warm-ups, and before matches. Repeating such affirmations will significantly effect your mentality and reshape your views and attitude.

## Step 4: Visualize Success

As you repeat your affirmations, add a layer of visualization. Picture yourself executing the perfect serve, winning matches, or achieving your tennis goals. This mental imagination can reinforce your affirmations and boost your confidence.

## Step 5: Flip the Script During Games

Finally, stay aware of your self-talk during games and competitions. When you notice negative self-talk creeping in, consciously replace it with your positive affirmations. This can eventually become a habit with consistent practice, resulting in improved performance, focus, and resilience on the tennis court.

## Remember..

Positive self-talk and affirmations are like mental muscles. The more you exercise them, the stronger they become, leading to increased mental toughness and improved performance.

# Visualization Power: Boosting Tennis Performance

In the intriguing world of sports psychology visualization, we have firsthand knowledge demonstrating how this potent tool can improve mental images and improve performance in tennis. Visualization, or mental imagery or rehearsal as it's also known, is all about cooking up detailed mental images of smashing it on the court. It's like a mental run-through of your moves, strategies, and actions on the court, paving the way to stellar performance and a champion's mindset. Let's explore the benefits of visualization, what it provides and how tennis players may incorporate it into their training.

Sport psychology gurus rave about visualization for a good reason. It's key because our mind is a big player in how we perform as athletes. What we think and imagine really impacts how we act and behave. Players may influence their ideas and beliefs by visualizing successful outcomes, fostering a positive mentality that improves their performance.

Visualization taps into our brain's knack for neuroplasticity, helping athletes to form new neural pathways that aid better physical execution and skill growth.

There's a whole list of perks when it comes to using visualization in tennis. First of all, it greatly boosts confidence. The players strengthen their confidence and assurance as they develop vivid mental pictures of making those shots, moving strategically, and gaining points.

This newfound confidence gives a big boost to their court performance, making them bolder, more focused, and able to bring their A-game.

Visualization also amps up concentration and focus. Players may train their brains to stay in the moment, anticipate what will happen, and make snap decisions by mentally going through several match scenarios.. This mental prep arms them with more clarity and coolness to face whatever a tennis match throws their way. Plus, visualization fine-tunes technique and motor skills.

When you mentally practice your strokes, footwork, and timing, your muscle memory improves, reaffirming the right approaches and enabling quicker, more accurate movements when you're actually playing.

It's also a stressbuster and anxiety-reliever. By mentally practicing tough situations, like going up against formidable opponents or facing key points, players can gear up mentally and emotionally. This lowers performance anxiety and helps them to tackle these situations with a cool-headed approach. Positive feelings are also generated by visualization, which boost the game's pleasure and fulfillment.

To get visualization working for them, tennis players should carve out regular practice sessions for this technique. Find a peaceful, comfy spot where you can focus completely without any interruptions. Close your eyes and bring all your senses into the visualization process. Imagine yourself standing on a tennis court, listening to the ball sound, holding racket in your hand, and enjoying the thrill of game.

Consistency and repetition may be your best buddies here. Make visualization a daily ritual by weaving it into your pre-practice or pre-match routine. Visualize various scenarios, including various court surfaces, opponents, and match situations. Concentrate on the little things, like the path the ball took, the bustle of the audience, and the way your movements felt in your body.

Visualization activities can facilitate tennis players boost their performance and mental focus. Athletes may develop confidence, concentration, improve strategies, and lower stress by developing specific mental visualization of excellent results. By folding visualization into their training routine, tennis players can unlock their mind's potential and let their talent shine on the court. Embrace the practice of visualization, harness the power of your imagination, and watch your tennis performance soar to new heights.

## Mindset Exercise: The Art of Visualization

### Step 1: Create Your Visualization Space

Find a quiet and comfortable spot where you can focus without interruptions. Here, you'll begin your visualization practice.

### Step 2: Engage All Your Senses

Close your eyes and engage all your senses. Consider the tennis court, the noise of the ball striking the racket, the feeling of your grasp, the flavour of your winning drink, as well as the aroma of fresh tennis balls. This full sensory experience makes your visualization more vivid and impactful.

### Step 3: Visualize Your Performance

Now, visualize yourself playing the perfect match. See yourself executing every stroke flawlessly, moving fluidly, outwitting your opponent, and ultimately, winning the game. Don't rush through this process. Take a moment to visualize each element and really absorb yourself in the environment.

## Step 4: Incorporate Different Scenarios

Practice visualizing various scenarios. Picture yourself playing on different court surfaces, against diverse opponents, and in different match situations. This variety will assist in sharpening your mind for any circumstance you might discover yourself in.

## Step 5: Add Relaxation Techniques

Include some deep breathing exercises in your routine along with your practise of visualization. This combination can improve your ability to concentrate and relax, as well as the efficacy of your imagination practice as a whole.

## Step 6: Practice Regularly

Consistency is key with visualization. Make it a daily ritual, incorporating it into your pre-practice or pre-match routine. The more often you visualize, the stronger the neural pathways associated with your envisioned actions become.

In its simplest form, visualisation may be an effective technique for improving tennis performance. You may boost your self-assurance, enhance your attention, get more proficient in your technique, and reduce anxiety if you create comprehensive mental representations of your game. Start practicing visualization today and see your tennis performance reach new heights.

# Visualization Magic: Enhancing Tennis Performance

In this chapter involving relaxation and energizing techniques, you will learn about the profound effects of managing stress, maintaining composure, and improving performance on the tennis court. We will explore the importance of implementing relaxation exercises and energizing techniques specifically tailored for tennis players. You can effectively handle stress, enhance your concentration, raise your motivation, and ultimately realise your full potential on the court if you include these techniques into your routine and make it a part of your daily routine.

## Relaxation techniques:

The ability to manage stress is critical to optimal tennis performance. Your ability to pay attention, make decisions, and perform well as a whole may all be adversely affected by stress. By implementing relaxation techniques, you can reduce stress levels and cultivate a sense of calm. You can manage your heart rate and trigger your body's innate relaxation response by practising deep breathing methods, such as diaphragm breathing, which enable you to control your breathing.

Progressive muscle relaxation involves consciously contracting and then releasing different muscle groups to release physical tension and induce deep relaxation. Guided imagery is another powerful technique that creates vivid images of calming and peaceful scenes to help calm the mind and reduce stress. Incorporating these relaxation exercises into your pregame routine, timeouts, and moments of high stress can help you stay calm and centered on the court, making clearer decisions and performing at your best.

## Energizing Techniques:

Energizing techniques are vital in increasing focus and motivation during intense competition. It is essential to construct a toolbox of various techniques that, when called upon, can invigorate both your mind and your body. Your muscles will be activated, and your body will be prepared for the game's physical demands when participating in a physical warm-up that includes dynamic mobility and stretching exercises.

Engaging in sensory activation can also be very effective in boosting energy levels. For example, listening to energizing music can stimulate your auditory senses and increase your alertness.

Incorporating aromatherapy into your daily life, such as breathing in the stimulating aroma of essential oils, may also benefit your state of mind and overall energy level.

Positive self-talk and visualizing successful accomplishments are mental techniques that can ignite your motivation and improve your mental focus. You may connect with your inner drive and direct your energy towards achieving your objectives if you maintain an encouraging mental attitude and create visual representations of yourself functioning at your very best.

Incorporate these energizing techniques into your pre-game rituals and changeovers to stay mentally and physically energized throughout the game, allowing you to maintain high performance and confidently overcome challenges.

You could connect with your inner drive and direct your energy towards achieving your goals if you maintain an optimistic mental attitude and create mental representations of yourself operating at your best. Incorporating relaxation exercises will help you manage stress and maintain composure, while energizing techniques will increase focus and motivation. You will be able to improve your calmness, lower your performance anxiety, and access your inner resources if you include these strategies into your everyday routine as well as your match-day prep. This will allow you to play at the highest level on the court.

### Remember..

Finding the right balance between relaxation and energizing techniques is key to unlocking your inner potential and reaching new heights in your tennis journey.

You can capitalize on the power of relaxing and energizing techniques to improve your skills, increase the amount of pleasure you get out of the game, and thrive on the court if you put in the right training and effort.

## Pro Athlete Power: Mindfulness & Meditation

Welcome aboard! You're about to embark on a journey exploring the immense goodness of mindfulness and meditation, specifically tailored for professional athletes, and you tennis pros, I'm looking at you!

In this chapter, we will go deeply into meditation and mindfulness and uncover the hidden potential of these strategies to improve your performance and overall well-being. Get ready to let out the power within you, cultivate a mentality comparable to zen, and thrive both on and off the tennis court.

The magic of meditation for professional athletes: In the high-stakes world of professional sports, the pressures can get crazy intense, physically and mentally. Here's where meditation steps in like a superhero. You can acquire expert-level self-awareness, attention, and mental fortitude via consistent meditation training.

Meditation is like a serene island that allows you to cultivate a calm and composed mind, helping you navigate stormy situations with a cool head. It offers a precious corner for introspection, assisting you in shedding limiting beliefs, busting mental blocks, and maximizing your potential as a professional athlete.

## The wonders of mindfulness and meditation:

The rewards of mindfulness and meditation for pro athletes are seriously impressive. To begin, these drills enhance your ability to concentrate and focus, making it easier to block out distractions and fully take part in each moment you spend on the court. In addition, they are very effective stress relievers, and they may help you deal with the pressures of competition and keep a healthy mental balance. On top of that, meditation builds resilience, helping you bounce back from slip-ups, stay fired up, and consistently bring your A-game. These practices also strengthen your mind-body connection, enhancing body awareness, coordination, and smooth movement.

## How to make these techniques work for you:

To weave meditation into your routine as a pro athlete, start with a basic technique like focused breathing. Make it a point to give yourself some alone time every day, during which you may just sit quietly and focus on your breathing. Allow your thoughts to come and go as they want without getting fixated on them, and bring your attention back to your breath if you find that it has strayed.

Body scan meditation is another potent technique that systematically explores sensations in different body parts, encouraging relaxation and physical awareness. Visualization meditation, where you imagine smashing performances, can also work wonders, laying neural pathways that beef up your confidence and on-court execution.

Meditation and mindfulness go hand in hand. Mindfulness is practicing paying attention to the here and now without attaching oneself to any particular thought or feeling. Incorporating mindfulness and meditation into athletes' routines can sharpen their ability to manage anxiety and perform under pressure.

Athletes benefit from mindfulness because it enables them to center themselves better, become more self-aware, and have a better hold on their thoughts and emotions. Body scanning and focusing on the breath are two examples of mindfulness exercises.

## Athlete's Mindfulness: A Step-by-Step Exercise

### Step 1: Find your zen spot

Choose a tranquil, quiet spot where you can practice without disturbances.

### Step 2: Get comfy

Find a comfortable sitting posture for you, whether on the floor or on a chair. Maintain a straight back while allowing your body to become relaxed.

### Step 3: Focus on your breath

Close your eyes and focus on your breathing. Take note of how each inhale and exhale feels in your body. If your mind drifts, gently steer it back to your breath.

## Step 4: Body scan

Gradually bring your awareness to different body parts, starting from your toes and moving up to your head. Notice any sensations or tension and consciously relax those areas as you breathe.

## Step 5: Let thoughts drift

Just let whatever ideas come to mind come and go without judging them. If your thoughts get caught in one another, gently direct your attention back to your breathing or the moment that is occurring right now.

## Step 6: Practice gratitude

Take a moment to reflect on what you're grateful for in your athletic journey. Cultivating gratitude can shift your perspective and promote a positive mindset.

## Step 7: Set intentions

Before wrapping up your workout, set positive intentions for your upcoming performance. Imagine yourself playing with reliability, focus, and delight.

## Consistency is key:

Make mindfulness and meditation a daily ritual. Even a few minutes of practice daily can make a big difference in managing anxiety and boosting performance.

By integrating these mindfulness and meditation practices into their daily routine, athletes can cultivate enhanced self-awareness, emotional control, and resilience. Athletes are equipped with a firm foundation for controlling anxiety and producing optimal results both on and off the pitch due to these strategies.

## Remember..

 Remember that this is not a race; it's a marathon. On this path to becoming a master of the inner game, remember to be patient with yourself and be nice to yourself so that you can experience the full advantages of your efforts.

# Nailing it When the Pressure's On: Techniques for Peak Performance.

Every athlete is challenged to perform at their absolute best when the heat is on. Staying cool, keeping focused, and pulling out top-tier performances in high-stakes situations can set athletes a cut above the rest. Here's a toolbox of techniques to help athletes nail it under pressure:

## Turn the pressure into a chance:

Instead of treating pressure as a weight to bear, athletes can turn it on its head and see it as a shot to show what they're made of. Athletes are able to change their worried energy into positive drive by shifting their mentality and viewing the pressure they are under as a challenge rather than a danger.

## Harness visualization and mental imagery:

Visualization is a super tool for athletes to test their performance and build confidence mentally. Athletes can visualize themselves doing each action flawlessly, making optimal judgments, and achieving their objectives. Athletes may boost their self-belief and alleviate some of the edge of their performance anxiety by replaying the moments of victory that have brought them the most success.

## Set up a pre-game routine:

Establishing a pre-game routine can help athletes settle their nerves and create a feeling of familiarity and control. This routine might include physical warm-ups, mental prep techniques like visualization or affirmations, and relaxation exercises. Before each performance, following a set pattern may instill a sense of self-assurance and make one feel more prepared.

## Stay in the moment and focused:

Staying present and keeping your eye on the ball is crucial in high-pressure situations. Athletes can train themselves to stay in the moment with mindfulness techniques.

Athletes may prevent their minds from straying to distractions or bad thoughts by concentrating on the here and now. This allows them to perform clearly and focus on what they are doing.

## Adopt a growth mindset:

Embracing a growth mindset means seeing challenges and setbacks as learning and growth opportunities. Athletes with a growth mindset get that failure and setbacks are just part of the journey to success. Athletes may maintain their drive and resiliency by transforming their failures into opportunities for growth and turning their losses into stepping stones on the path to better.

**Rally your support crew:**

When things start to become intense, athletes must have a community of people they can count on for support. Having someone you can bounce ideas off of and talk about your concerns with may bring vital insight and reassurance, regardless of whether that person is a coach, a teammate, or a sports psychologist. Open communication can reduce anxiety and help athletes feel backed up and understood.

**Try relaxation techniques:**

Practicing relaxation techniques, like deep breathing, progressive muscle relaxation, or meditation, can help athletes manage their body's responses to pressure. These techniques encourage a calm state and help ease tension and anxiety, letting athletes perform with greater ease and a clear mind.

Athletes may develop the mental toughness and abilities necessary to perform well under pressure if they give these approaches and strategies a go and give it their best attempt. Remember that adapting these strategies to your unique needs is essential to determine which are most successful. With practice and grit, athletes can tap into the power of pressure to crank their performance up a notch.

## Mastering the Zone: Focus Techniques in Tennis

In the intricate game of tennis, the ability to focus is a critical skill that can make the difference between clutching the trophy and sulking in defeat. This chapter highlights stepping up your concentration game and giving distractions the cold shoulder on the tennis court. By trying these approaches and ideas, athletes may develop the mental fortitude and abilities necessary to excel under pressure. Don't forget that it's essential to tailor these strategies to your unique needs and determine which are most effective for you.

## Why's focus such a big deal for tennis players?

Honing your focus is a game-changer in tennis for a bunch of reasons. First, it allows you to be smack-dab in the present moment, helping you read the game like a book, anticipate your opponent's moves, and react pronto. Next, a laser-focused mind ramps up your mental balance, letting you stay cool as a cucumber even when the heat's cranked up. Finally, it acts as a barrier between you and potential sources of distraction, such as the clamour of the crowd, other external variables, or nagging negative thoughts. This makes it easier for you to maintain your eyes on the ball and perform at your peak throughout the entirety of the game.

Stepping up your focus offers a ton of goodies to tennis players. It pumps up shot consistency and accuracy and slashes unforced errors.

Players are able to enter the zone, make split-second decisions, execute shots with pinpoint precision, and adjust on the fly to changes in the game dynamics when they increase their attention and mental intensity. A better awareness of one's body is another benefit of concentrating more intently, as it enables players to improve their footwork, timing, and general coordination.

To get these focus-boosting techniques working for you, tennis players can try these strategies:

## Lock in a pre-point routine:

Whip up a personal routine before each point to prime your mind for max focus. This routine can include deep breathing exercises to center yourself, visualizing winning shots, and reminding yourself of key tactical tips or strategies.

Maintain your focus on the work at hand by bringing your attention to the here and now as well as the activity immediately in front of you. Don't allow the score or the results of the future to distract you. Focus on the task at hand. Maintaining a proactive game plan while focusing on precisely landing each shot should be your primary concern.

## Master attention control:

Get good at staying focused despite distractions around you. Train yourself to refocus quickly after each point, ignoring the racket from the crowd, your opponent's antics, or other external factors that can steal your focus. Build up the skill to stay mentally dialed-in and in the zone.

## Boost the mind-body connection:

Nurture a strong mind-body link by staying in tune with your physical sensations during the game. Maintain concentration on your breathing, the sensation of the racket in your hand, and the movements of your body. Keeping your mind firmly planted in the here and now can assist you in maintaining your concentration and preventing distractions from throwing you off your game.

## Dive into Mental Rehearsals:

Before matches, get into mental rehearsals to simulate various game situations and practice maintaining focus and concentration.

Picture yourself staying cool-headed, flawlessly pulling off your game plan, and successfully tackling hurdles. This mental rehearsal will improve your capacity to concentrate and perform well under pressure.

By making these techniques a regular part of training and match play, tennis players can ramp up their focus, give distractions the boot, and improve their on-court performance. Keep in mind that increasing your focus is a process that will take time and will require dedication, practise, and an attitude of mindfulness. Tennis players can improve their skills and reach their potential if they put in significant work and maintain a sharp focus.

## From Doubt to Belief: Tennis Confidence Building

Howdy! Let's dive into the role of confidence and handling expectations in making or breaking a tennis player's game. This chapter focuses on building confidence and successfully juggling performance expectations. When times are tough, we'll also walk you through several smart tactics that will help you maintain confidence in your capabilities and strengthen your ability to bounce back. By giving these techniques a whirl, you can cultivate a rock-solid mental foundation to level up your tennis game.

Confidence is the bedrock of success in tennis. It allows players to trust their abilities, make calls on the fly, and precisely nail those shots. When you have confidence in yourself and your abilities, you are more likely to take risks, rise to the occasion, and deliver your best possible performance. Along the same lines, handling performance expectations like a pro is vital for keeping a healthy mindset.

Having unrealistically high expectations might put unreasonable pressure on you, which can negatively affect your performance. On the other hand, having reasonable expectations helps promote a positive mentality and increases the enjoyment that can be enjoyed while playing the game.

The perks of confidence and managing expectations like a boss: Pumping up your confidence and nailing expectation management has a heap of perks for tennis players. First off, beefed-up confidence ramps up focus, decision-making, and shot execution, leading to better overall performance. When you have faith in your skills, you are more likely to focus on the here and now, have faith in your instincts, and provide your best performance. Secondly, by managing expectations like a pro, players can dial down stress and anxiety, enabling them to perform with more chill and composure. Players are able to approach games with a clear and focused attitude when their expectations are realistic and when those expectations match their talents. In addition, having self-assurance and setting reasonable goals helps create mental toughness, which enables athletes to recover quickly from mental setbacks and have a positive view even when confronted with challenges.

Recognizing and praising oneself for one's accomplishments, capabilities, and talents is essential in developing one's self-confidence. Take some time off to think about your accomplishments and refresh your memory on what you're capable of. Set realistic, doable goals that stretch your abilities and gradually build confidence.

Imagine yourself pulling off a successful performance, visualizing the feelings, emotions, and positive outcomes tied to your top performances. Use positive affirmations to bolster your belief in your abilities and silence any doubts that might creep in. Challenges should be welcomed, and they should be viewed, rather than as failures, as opportunities for growth and improvement.

Handling performance expectations involves setting realistic goals based on your current skill set and progress. Put the spotlight on the journey rather than the destination, emphasizing the effort, improvement, and joy you get from playing tennis.

Break down big goals into bite-sized, more doable steps to stay stoked and track your progress. Adopt a growth mindset, viewing slip-ups and setbacks as precious learning opportunities that can fuel your growth.

This frame of mind enables you to approach obstacles with an attitude of curiosity and resilience, which enables you to recover from failure and continue to develop as a player.

By boosting your confidence and adopting a realistic and positive mindset, you can step up your performance, maintain mental resilience, and truly love the game of tennis. Try techniques covered in this chapter, such as determining your best qualities, establishing attainable goals, visualizing yourself achieving success, and adopting a growth mindset. With consistent practice and faith in your abilities, your confidence will skyrocket and your game will hit new heights.

## Emotional Resilience: Mental Strength in Tennis

Tennis players face a roller coaster of pressure, hiccups, and emotional highs and lows, making emotional resilience a must-have trait. This chapter is all about putting light on the role that emotional resilience plays in tennis, highlighting the advantages that it delivers, and giving a toolset of practical tactics that can be used to foster and strengthen this essential mental ability.

## Getting to Grips with the Importance of Emotional Resilience:

In the cutthroat world of tennis, emotional resilience is vital for keeping your eyes on the ball, handling stress, and bouncing back from a loss. Even when the going gets rough, it offers athletes the edge they need to maintain their composure, make judgments with clarity of thought, and deliver their finest performance. Emotional resilience gears players up to roll with the punches, recover from slip-ups, and keep their spirits high throughout matches and tournaments.

## Perks of Emotional Resilience:

Building emotional resilience has a heap of perks for tennis players. First, it ramps their ability to handle pressure like a pro, dialling down anxiety and stepping up performance when under stress. Resilient players are more likely to bounce back in no time from losses, keeping their confidence and motivation levels high. In addition, having a high level of emotional resilience helps to improve one's emotional well-being, which in turn reduces the danger of burnout and enhances one's general mental health. Players are better able to manage disagreement and have a positive viewpoint in the face of intense competition, which in turn builds their relationships not just with their teammates but also with their coaches and their opponents.

## Getting Emotional Resilience into Gear

**Tuning into Emotions**: Foster self-awareness by pinpointing and understanding your emotions during practice and game time. Pay attention to how different scenarios impact your emotional state so you can react appropriately and make wise calls.

## Managing Emotions:

Hone techniques to effectively regulate and manage your emotions. Deep breathing, visualization, and progressive muscle relaxation can help you keep cool and focus, even in high-stakes moments.

Integrating these strategies into your pre-match routine can help you feel more at ease and give you a clear head start.

## Self-reflection:

Carve out time for regular self-reflection to spot patterns in emotional responses and areas that need a bit of work. You may gain some useful insights for your personal development by reflecting on earlier performances and analysing how your feelings influenced how you played.

## The Bottom Line:

Building emotional resilience is an ongoing journey for tennis players. Players can tackle the game's challenges with confidence and mental toughness by recognizing the importance of emotional resilience, tapping into its benefits, and using practical strategies.

Players will be able to maintain their calm, cope with stress, and perform with a clear head and attention if they cultivate an awareness of their emotions and develop skills for regulating those emotions. Players that are able to flourish in the face of adversity, maximise their potential, and enjoy a satisfying and successful tennis career are those who have developed emotional resilience as their anchor.

# Techniques to thrive and perform at the highest level under pressure

Delivering a top-notch performance under pressure is a hurdle every athlete has to jump. The knack to keep cool, focus, and perform at your absolute best when high stakes can make you stand out from the crowd. Here's a playbook of techniques to help you nail it when under pressure:

## Flip the script on pressure:

Instead of lugging pressure around as a burden, athletes can flip the script and see it as a golden opportunity to show off their skills and step up their game.

Athletes can transform their restless energy into a surge of positive motivation by adjusting their mentality and reframing pressure as a challenge rather than a bogeyman in their imaginations.

## Get in on visualization and mental imagery:

Visualization is a potent tool for athletes to practice their performance and pump up confidence mentally. Athletes can create vibrant mental movies of themselves nailing smooth movements, making pinpoint decisions, and smashing their goals. Athletes may boost their self-belief and tone down their performance nerves by mentally recreating times when they were successful in their competition.

## Craft a pre-performance ritual:

Setting up a pre-performance ritual can help athletes tame their nerves and create a sense of familiarity and control. This rite could consist of physical warm-ups, mental preparation tactics like visualising or affirming your goals, and other practises to help you calm out. Having a structured routine before each performance can brew a sense of confidence and readiness.

## Keep your head in the game:

The knack for staying present and focused is key when the pressure's on. Athletes can school themselves to stay in the present moment with mindfulness techniques. Athletes may prevent their minds from straying off to distractions or negative ideas by anchoring their attention to the here and now. This enables them to execute with clarity and focus, which benefits their overall performance.

## Embrace a growth mindset:

Rocking a growth mindset means seeing challenges and setbacks as chances for learning and growth. Athletes with a growth mindset get that failure and setbacks are just stepping stones on the path to success. Athletes are able to recover more effectively and maintain sky-high levels of enthusiasm and resiliency if they view setbacks as launch pads for progress rather than as reasons to give up.

## Lean on your support network:

It's key for athletes to have a support squad they can lean on when the pressure's mounting. Having someone to depend on and talk about one's concerns with, whether it be a coach, a teammate, or a sports shrink, may provide one with crucial insights and reassurance. Open chat can lower anxiety and help athletes feel backed and understood.

## Give relaxation techniques a shot:

Dipping into relaxation techniques, like deep breathing, progressive muscle relaxation, or meditation, can help athletes manage their bodily responses to pressure. Athletes are able to compete with better comfort and a clearer mind when they use these strategies because they induce a feeling of calm and assist in minimizing stress and anxiety levels.

By putting these techniques and strategies into play, athletes can build the mental toughness and skills to smash it under pressure. Remember that it is essential to tailor these strategies to your needs and determine what works best for you. With practice and stick-to-itiveness, athletes can harness the power of pressure to kick their performance up a notch.

# Part 3 – Best Practices Before and During a Tennis Match

# Pre-Match Rituals and Techniques in Tennis

Alright, so we've got a big tennis match on the horizon. It can be nerve-wracking, can't it? The hours leading up to the match can feel like a whirlwind of emotions.

You're excited, you're nervous, you're prepared, and you're worried all at the same time. Everything is a complete and utter muddle. This is quite normal, and the following reasons will explain why.

Your body's gearing up for a showdown, friend. You're like a car revving its engine at the starting line, raring to go. It's possible that your surge of energy may make you feel like a roaring torrent. On the other hand, if you don't know how to direct it appropriately, it might become a tornado of anxious thoughts and feelings.

Many players believe the key is to sit and relax. They sit around playing cards or zoning out on the TV. That's like caging a wild animal - all that energy is trapped, desperate to escape. It's not the way to go, let me tell you.

Physical energy is not the issue. It's limitless, like a renewable energy source. What drains us is our own mind games - the negativity, the anxiety, the self-doubt. Now, in order to clear our minds, we can't always just go for a stroll in the woods, but there are things that we can do to combat energy overload.

What about playing some tennis casually with a buddy a couple of hours before the match? That's right, get out there, loosen up, practice those shots. No tennis courts? A wall will also do the trick.

You are not simply wasting time but keeping your body active and putting that excess energy to productive use.

No option for a physical warm-up? No problem. Lock yourself in your room, blast your favorite tunes, and shake a leg! Does that strike you as odd? But believe me, singing and dancing will cut through those nerves like a hot knife through butter. These fun activities have major therapeutic potential; the bonus is you're too busy feeling good to worry about the match.

And laughter, my friend, is your secret weapon. If you take things too seriously, you're going to freeze up. Laugh at yourself; laugh at the situation. Laughter relaxes your body and mind, putting you in the perfect state to ace the game.

From a mental standpoint, check your breathing when you start dwelling on the match. Relax, take it slow, and savour the moment. You should start imagining your previous victories on the court and recreate those winning moments and your greatest shots. Imagine yourself making those shots with complete accuracy and collecting points. See the look on your opponent's face - they can't touch you! You're the champ, and everyone knows it.

Think of this like studying for a role in a play. You need to know every scene, every expression, every line by heart. This way, you're ready to give a star performance. Visualization is like your secret practice session. It's proven to work wonders alongside your physical training.

If visualizing doesn't come naturally, pretend you're watching a movie. You are sitting in your favourite recliner, munching on some popcorn, and the main character in the movie are you, tearing it up on the tennis court. Believe me when I say that using this strategy will eventually become as natural as breathing to you, providing you with amazing results.

Listening to calming music, and visualization can also help create a state of tranquillity, putting you in harmony with yourself.

The main point here is to recognize when you start spiraling into negative thoughts and emotions. Take action immediately and channel the negative energy into something productive. When you get onto the court, keep your body relaxed while keeping your mind vigilant and confident. Remember, you've got this. Now go out there and serve some aces!

## What to Do During a Tennis Match

So, we've done the hard work, right? We're now set to get on the court and face anyone without fear. We're excited to bring all our practice into play and tackle this new test. We're ready to stay calm, keep our heads cool, and give our best shot.

But let's face the facts. Walking onto the court can sometimes feel like a lot. Especially when people are watching. When an actor walks out onto the stage for the first time, all eyes are on them, and so it is with this situation.

But remember what we talked about in Chapter One? We're not the nervousness or the thoughts buzzing around inside our heads. By taking some deep, slow breaths, we can connect with our true calm self, right there in our belly, just a little below the navel.

Because of this, we can enter the court victorious, exuding self-assurance from every pore of our bodies and displaying our individuality.

Remember our discussion about energy? You need to make sure that you occupy as much space as possible right off the off. Your opponent and anyone watching should feel your energy.

As soon as you begin to warm up, immediately direct all of your attention to your breathing, the movements you are performing, and the ball. Follow the ball wherever it goes, never taking your eyes off it or getting distracted. No matter what occurs during the match, you will remain focused and attentive thanks to this preparation.

The game is about ready to get underway. One of the questions that I constantly ask my students is what they're considering, what's currently going through their minds, and what they believe they need to be doing right now. The responses are frequently things like, "I need to score as many points as possible," "I must not make any mistakes," and "I want to win at all costs!"

But honestly, if you're thinking like this, winning becomes tough. The moment we start using phrases like "I have to" or "I want to," we immediately begin to put pressure on ourselves and experience increased levels of stress; nevertheless, these are the very things that we are attempting to steer clear of.

Thoughts such as "wanting to win at all costs" and "fear of losing" in particular may severely screw with us. Instead, I motivate myself by telling myself, "I'm here to watch the ball, do my exercises, focus on my breathing, stay centered and alert, and most importantly, have fun." I'm not only concerned with gaining victory or avoiding defeat in this competition. I came here to give it my all and play the best tennis I can.

By thinking like this, I don't focus on my opponent, the score, or anything happening off the court. All of these factors have the potential to divert my attention and impact the way I play. Instead, the match becomes like a kind of meditation, helping me stay aware and in the moment.

I stop seeing my opponent as a tough enemy to beat. Instead, they become more of a partner. If I didn't have them, I wouldn't be able to play, which would prevent me from improving my talents and putting them to the test. In fact, the level of interest in the game increases in proportion to how well they play. As we take on this brand-new and exciting task, we can demonstrate what we are capable of and possibly push ourselves farther than we have before.

There have been moments, particularly in the early rounds of a tournament when I realized my opponent was powerful and playing really well. Initially, I'd feel scared and unsure, but after realizing that those feelings won't help me play well, I started seeing my opponent differently. Not with fear but with respect. I started considering them as a "worthy opponent" who matched my ability and skills. And guess what? I actually started enjoying the challenge.

This is why we play matches and competitions if you think about it. It's a means for us to assess ourselves, evaluate what we're capable of, and win the internal game with ourselves.

When writing, remember to use a conversational and informal style. Be direct and straightforward, using everyday language and casual phrases to build a connection with the reader. Talk to them directly and keep them hooked throughout the text. Maintain a strong tone and a basic language to prevent seeming like AI-generated material and to make your writing more realistic and motivating to the reader.

## Making the Most of Breaks

Let's move to one of the most important bits of a match - changing courts. It's possible that you don't think this is that important but believe me when I say that it is.

It's super easy to let our attention wander when we're not actively playing, right? Maybe you start thinking about stuff happening off-court or start chatting with people you know. However, this may disrupt your ability to concentrate, making it more difficult to get back into the zone after the game has resumed. Hence, what do I do when the court is changing? I sit, close my eyes, and concentrate entirely on my breathing, both when inhaling and exhaling. I pay absolutely no attention to everything that is occurring around me.

I take a few sips of water, letting my body and muscles relax in sync with my breathing. It's almost like getting refueled, and it makes me feel just as amped up as I did when the match first started.

You may even use a towel to shut out everything else by wrapping it over your head and covering your face. You should utilize this time to psych yourself up if you're having trouble with the game you're playing. Repeat to yourself that you're strong, unstoppable, and winning. When you get back on the court, everyone will feel your power.

And here's a big rule of thumb - never rush. Missed the first shot? Don't hurry to play the next one. Instead, stop, center yourself, relax, regain your cool and confidence. Remember that you are there to play, enjoy yourself, and keep your attention on the ball at all times. Only start playing again when you're really ready. This is super important between points and during court changes.

Ever noticed how some players bounce the ball a few times before the first serve or straighten the racket strings between serves? These simple routines can help you remain calm, centered, and in control of the situation. They prevent you from letting your thoughts wander to the past or the future, keeping you grounded in the here and now. This prevents you from dwelling on the point you dropped or the easy shot you missed.

To take your mental game to the next level, you need to become your own coach. Be mindful of how you move your body and use your racket at the end of each stroke. It's about replaying your movements in your mind so clearly that it's like watching a movie.

Once you have it figured out, you may determine the mental or emotional factors that may have contributed to an error you made. Having this knowledge can assist you in regaining control of the situation and preventing your mind from wandering off into other ideas. Even things like wind can be used to your advantage. You may see it as a chance to focus even more intently on your workout and keep an eye on the ball, rather than seeing it as an interruption to your routine. It's about harnessing the things that used to throw you off to increase your ability to stay in the moment, whether you're on the court or not. This applies whether you're playing or not.

When you really stop and think about it, most mistakes are mental or emotional, even if they seem technical. The ability to comprehend what was happening in your head at the time of an error might be a decisive factor in the outcome of a situation.

The mind loves to try and control the body, giving it instructions it doesn't really need. However, the purpose of all the methods and exercises we have discussed so far is to completely remove the mind and emotions from the equation so that the body can function normally.

Consider the act of getting out of bed as an example. You know you don't have to give much thought to each step, right? You only need to make the decision to get up, and your body will do the rest. The same goes for things like breathing and walking. You want to bring this same ease to playing tennis. When you are making those strokes, you need to allow your body the freedom to move whatever it wants, even though you will have an idea of what to do in certain scenarios. It's not about winning; it's about letting go.

And here's one last tip to help with this: start singing. It makes no difference whether you say it out loud, under your breath, or to yourself in your brain. Singing helps clear your mind of thoughts and emotions. There's a lot of truth in the saying "Sing it out."

## About the author

David J. Fritz, Ph.D., is a sports psychologist passionate about tennis and a father of two teens in love with Nadal and Federer.

His experiences as a competitive tennis player, along with his passion for assisting other athletes in reaching their full potential, inspired him to pursue a career in sports psychology.

After extensive psychology studies, focusing particularly on performance, he authored the acclaimed book, "Mental Game of Tennis Players." This ground-breaking work is now considered required reading for athletes, coaches, and parents since it is filled with actionable ideas for improving mental toughness.

Beyond writing, Dr. Fritz is deeply committed to researching new ways to enhance mental toughness, intending to assist aspiring professional tennis players cultivate a winning mindset. His continuing contributions to sports psychology and the one-of-a-kind viewpoint he brings to the table as an athlete, a parent, and a psychologist continue to revolutionize how we perceive and approach mental toughness in sports.

## Your Free Gift

To thank you for your purchase, I've also put together your gift to download now online: A collection of worksheets to improve your mental and technical performance. A conducive framework that will help you make the most of your practice court time!

download.marketinga.club

## Leave a review

As an independent author with a small marketing budget, reviews are my livelihood on this platform. I would truly appreciate your honest opinion if you liked this book. I personally read every review because I like hearing from my readers.

### Thank you!

David J. Fritz

Made in the USA
Columbia, SC
04 May 2024

35261977R00061